ANATOMY FOR INTERIOR DESIGNERS

JULIUS PANERO, A.I.A., N.S.I.D.
ILLUSTRATIONS BY NINO REPETTO, DR. ARCH., M.S.
THIRD EDITION
WHITNEY LIBRARY OF DESIGN, NEW YORK

© 1948, 1951, 1962
Whitney Library of Design Division
Whitney Publications, Inc.
Charles E. Whitney, President
William Wilson Atkin, Vice-President
First edition 1948
Second edition 1951
Third edition 1962
Designed by Stephen Dwoskin
Printed in the United States of America.
Library of Congress Catalog Card No. 62-18472.

DEDICATION

This, the third edition of **Anatomy for Interior Designers,** is dedicated to the memory of Francis de N. Schroeder, former editor of Interiors magazine and author and compilator of the previous editions of this book.

That his untimely passing has deprived so many of his talents and subtle wit is indeed a sad loss. That we should be given the task of expanding upon his work is both an honor and a challenge.

TABLE OF CONTENTS

THE BASIS OF ALL DESIGN

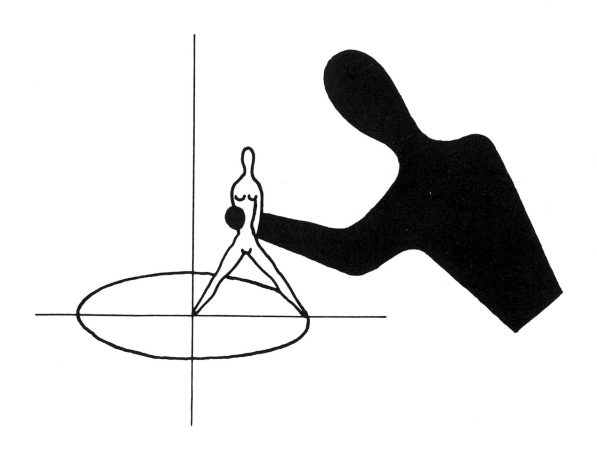

BASIC MEASUREMENTS

It has been said that no knowledge can be more satisfactory to a man than that of his own frame, its parts, their functions and actions. In addition to this rather sophisticated observation we might also add that the proportions of the human body are generally attractive to most of us, which accounts for the popularity of Jayne Mansfield, classical sculpture, and reducing pills. But let's face it—from an engineering point of view the human body really isn't the best of all possible machines. It cannot exist when the skin temperature varies more than six or seven degrees. It cannot hibernate, and it cannot regularly fly south for the winter unless it belongs to a retired millionaire or gangster. It is also a fault of the human body, as a machine, that it cannot curl up like a snake or hang from a tree by its tail and that it only bends in three or four places. Due to these rather obvious inadequacies man was forced to conceive of two protective devices, namely, clothing and architecture. From architecture, the human mind developed the refinement of furniture.

It was because of all these problems that man also published the first and second edition of this book and is now giving vent to this third and greatly enlarged edition which contains much material not previously discussed. For the most part, this latest edition, like the previous two, is predicated on the thesis that man is the measure of all things and it consequently contains many additional useful measurements and design criteria. Moreover, the book has been reorganized for easier reference and contains several completely new sections. The purpose of this third book, like the purpose of the last two, is to help you think for yourself.

MAN IS THE MEASURE OF ALL THINGS

The proportions of the human body are the basis of all design. One of the first to state this fact was Pythagoras of Samos who wrote the inscription that appears at the top of the opposite page. Translated it reads, "Man is the Measure of all Things." Many years later Euclid restated the same thing in the mathematical formula also reproduced here, and in the 15th century Leonardo Da Vinci illustrated Euclid's formula (which by now was known as "The Golden Rule") with the diagram of the man's body inside the circle and square.

Proper application of Euclid's Golden Rule, the relation of alpha to sigma, should enable you to design almost anything from a radio to a ballroom and have it in correct proportion. But it really isn't necessary to know much about algebra, plane geometry, or Euclid in order to design furniture correctly in its relation to the human body. Others, some using higher mathematics and more using simple trial and error, have done this work for us.

For the information in the following pages we have gone to designers, architectural reference books, and in one or two cases to life insurance statistics to present our own table of standards. For easy reference these standards relate to the normal activities of an average man or woman through the course of an average day at home, in the office, and socializing with friends.

πάντων χρημάτων
μέτρον ἄνθρωπος

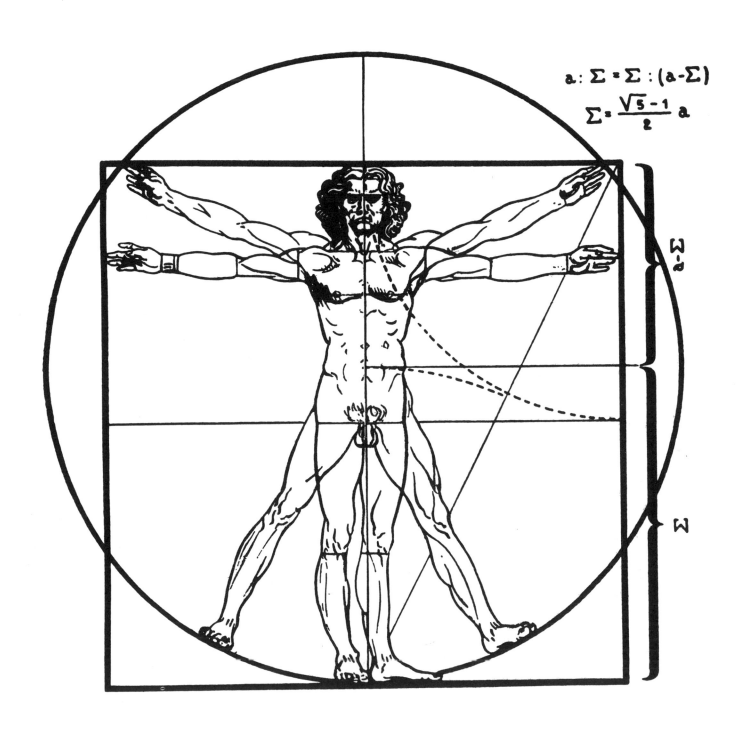

$a : \Sigma = \Sigma : (a - \Sigma)$

$\Sigma = \dfrac{\sqrt{5} - 1}{2}\, a$

It is impossible to paint a picture without knowing something about the fundamentals of human anatomy, but as our artist has suggested, it is also impossible to design a chair without knowing something about the human fundamentals. Even so, there are too many uneasy chairs on the market, beds that a body can't turn over in, and tables that turn over too easily. Most of the things that designers need to know about space and the human body can be found on the pages that follow, whether it be the maximum heights to build reachable shelving or the angle of incidence of a poke in the nose.

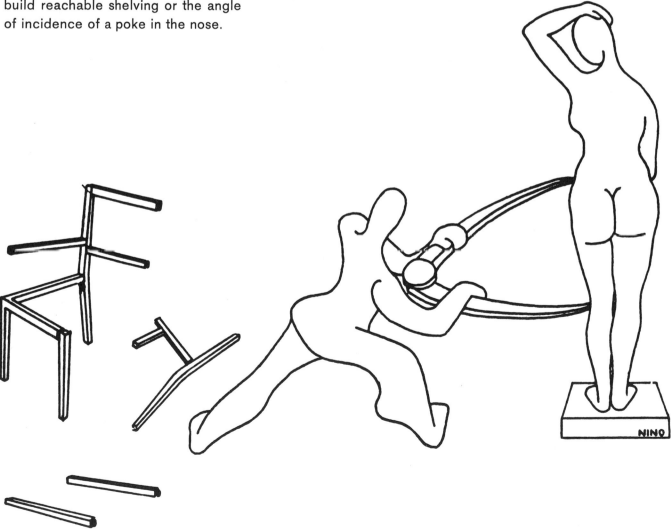

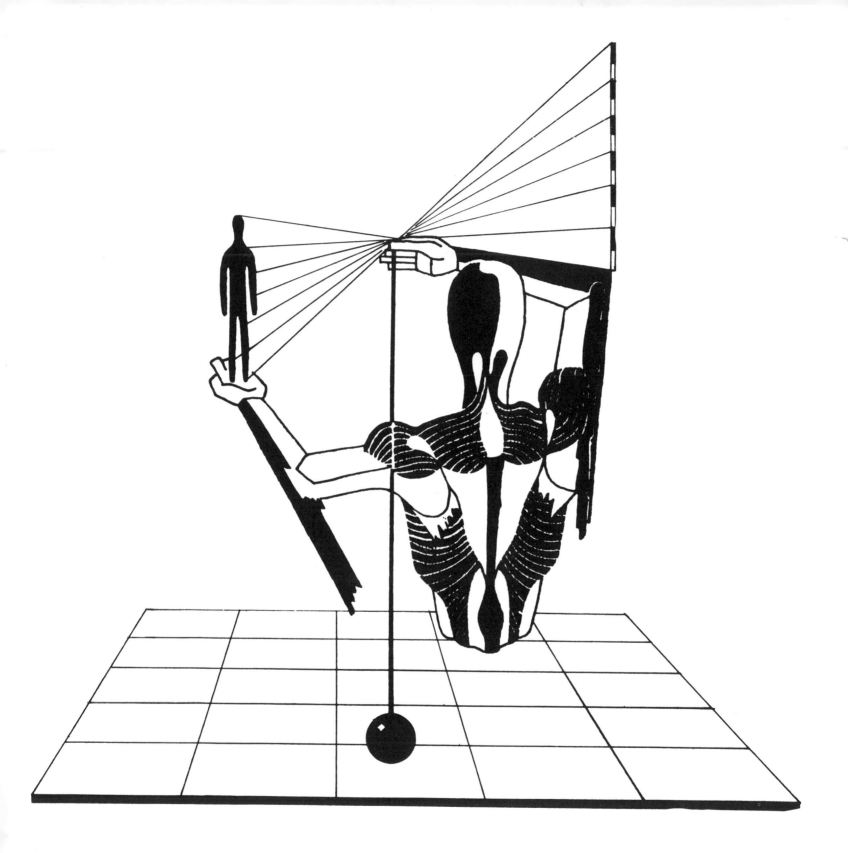

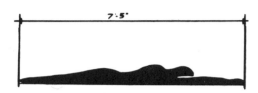

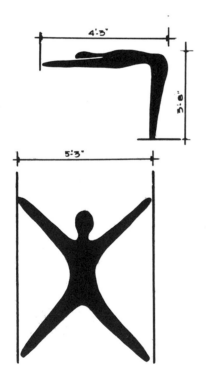

The next pages contain most of the fundamental measurements any designer needs to know and the ensuing pages analyze and amplify them. We call your attention to the group of drawings on this page which constitute a sort of paraphrase of the original Leonardo drawing.

Among other important facts they include the full extension of a yawning man, a prostrate corpse, a lady engaged in reducing exercises and someone spreadeagled in the attitude of Leonardo.

The drawings on the opposite page contain a designer's entire notebook of useful measurements. Make a game of it and see if you can identify some of the following gems: The amount of side space necessary to dry yourself comfortably with a bath towel, to find out how hot the tub is, and to brush your teeth; the width necessary for two people to squeeze past each other in a narrow corridor, and to pass each other comfortably; the space occupied by four policemen guarding a department store door, four lady shoppers trying to get in, and four pickets on the march; the area occupied by a male quartet in full song; four ways for a railroad porter to carry one or two suitcases; the height of a pontoon bridge guard rail, and the work surface of a sewing machine; the space occupied by a passive onlooker; a man with a wheelbarrow; a Broadway wolf about to make a proposition; the correct height at which to weed a garden, bake a pie, and wash dishes; the highest shelf on which to stack dishes without breaking them; the clearances needed in designing rows of theatre seats so that people may see over each others heads and pass each other between the rows; the smallest dressing room in which three chorus girls can put their clothes off and on; the proper heights of an index card file; the average heights of people from infancy to 19 year old basketball players.

RESIDENTIAL APPLICATIONS

It is sad indeed that the unknown genius who invented the chair has not reaped the historical acclaim befitting such a significant contribution to the comfort of man. As proof of the greatness of his creation it should be noted that since the third dynasty in Egypt the proportions of a good chair, be it a side chair, arm chair or electric chair, have not varied greatly from those shown here.

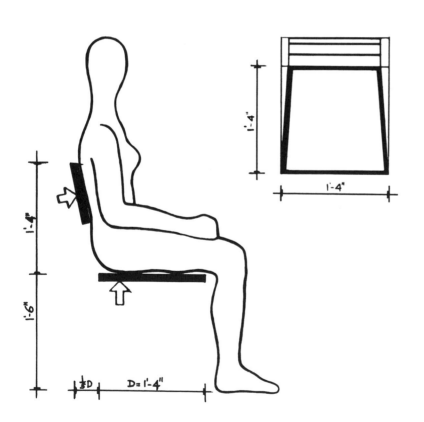

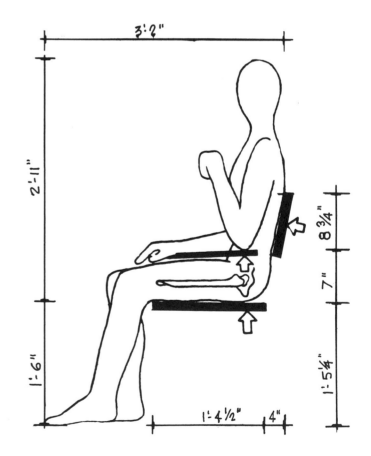

Minimum dimensions from the standard side and arm chair showing points of greatest strain. Note that the distance from the top of the chair back is one fifth the depth of the seat.

THE LIVING ROOM

In the arrangement of any home, space tends to be allocated for two different kinds of use—specialized and general. The specialized uses include activities like sleeping, cooking and bathing for which we have specialized rooms such as bedrooms, kitchens, and bathrooms. General use, however, tends to center in one room—the living room. The small drawing above, has symbolized some—but by no means all—of the activities which that room accommodates in the normal course of events. Sharp eyes will discern a cigarette, a drink, an open book, a radio, a television set, the ace of clubs, and a mouthful of teeth for talking and eating. Put them all together and you have still another very important activity to which the living room must adapt itself: entertaining. These activities, or their equivalents are as old as mankind and man has allotted the largest room in the house to them ever since he began to build dwellings of more than one room.

In recent years because of high construction costs and the evermounting desire to devise a plan that will circumvent the cramping psychological effect of restricted dimensions, we have tended toward what architects call "open planning" for living space. This concept is by no means new, starting back in the great hall of a medieval barony and continuing through the comfortably-sized nineteenth century house in a wavering but unmistakable line to the Park Avenue duplex and the converted Connecticut barn.

One of the arguments against the open plan that has been gaining in support is the lack of privacy for the dining area.

The two schematic diagrams of the open plan living room show the organization of space to be vertical as well as horizontal with the living space extending the full height of the two floors.

Still another variation of the open plan is to eliminate the vertical organization of space but maintain the horizontal relationships illustrated. This approach is quite common in one-story houses.

The theory of the open plan living space is to build as few permanent partitions as possible, and to separate visually the dining area from the main section, as well as to give access to the patio or garden which is as important in today's living as it was in the time of Louis XIV.

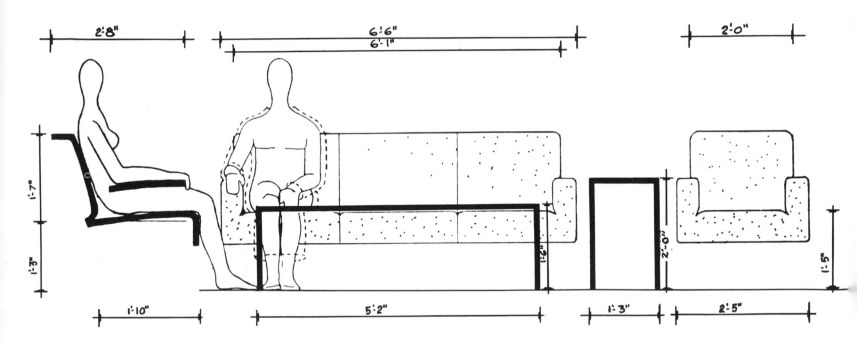

Standard proportions for easy chairs, couch, end table, and a long magazine table, useful for offices as well as for private living rooms. Note particularly the height of arms above the upholstered seat.

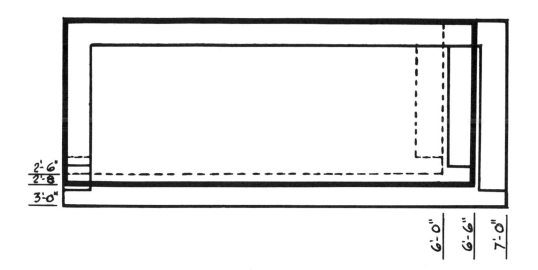

2'-6"
2'-8"
3'-0"

6'-0"
6'-6"
7'-0"

Sofas, day beds, and couches generally come in the three sizes illustrated above. A seven foot couch is necessary if people are to sleep on it. Top measurements of the end table and long magazine table are shown below.

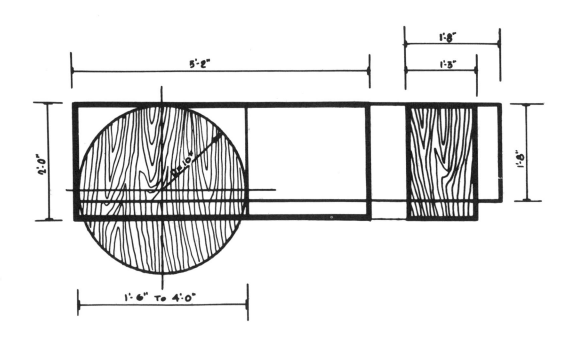

1'-8"
1'-3"
5'-2"
2'-0"
1'-8"
1'-6" To 4'-0"

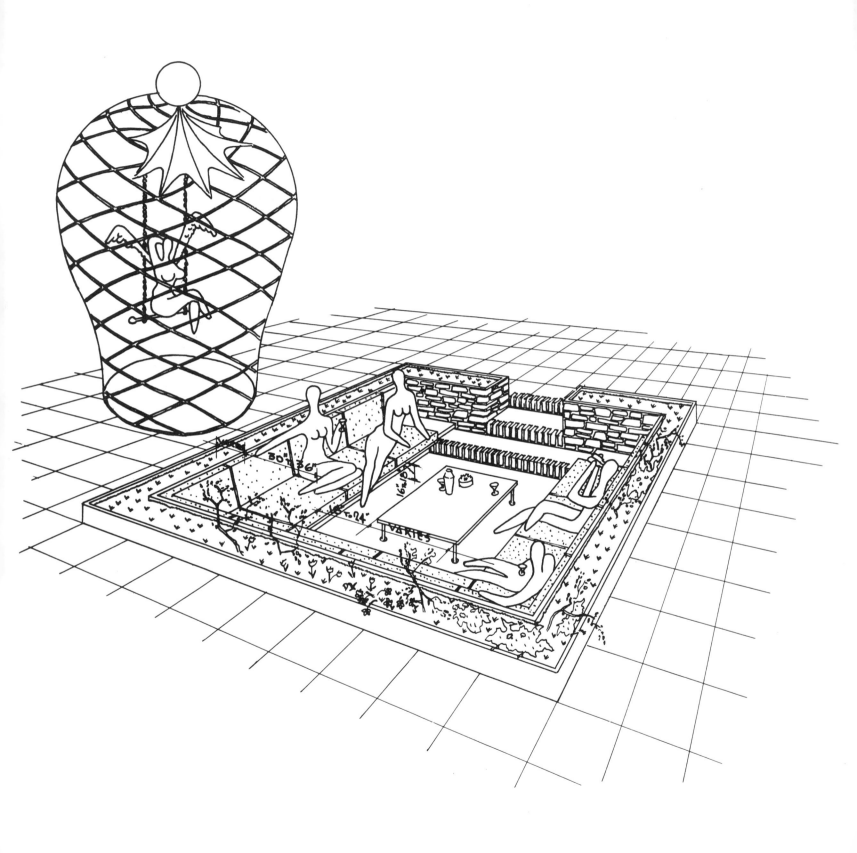

By now every interior designer knows the importance of conversational groups in the layout of living rooms, lounges, club rooms, etc. A conversational group, in design parlance, is the familiar two chairs and coffee table in front of the fireplace; the arrangements around a card table or a grand piano, and so on to that latest development, the conversation pit.

The figure at right illustrates the so-called "arc of conversation" within which conversation is comfortable, and also includes such important measurements as the proper knee space between chairs and tables; what is meant by "within arm's reach"; and the right size for a coffee table. The basic data contained in this illustration can be translated with some slight modification to the minimum requirements for the design of one of the more recent additions to conversational groupings —the "conversation pit" shown opposite.

The figures overleaf contain 32 diagrams which indicate the space required for the objects used in the living room.

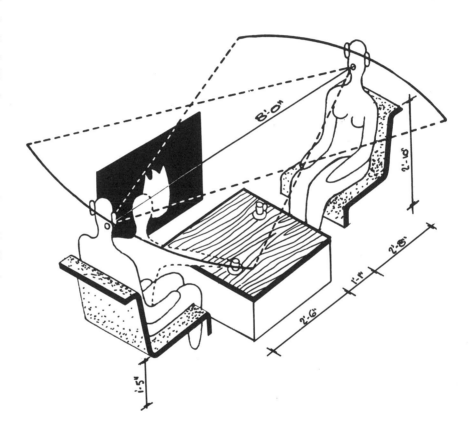

The arc of conversation, the distance at which people sit without feeling either constrained or remote.

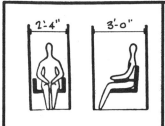 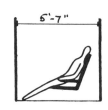 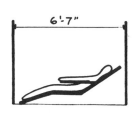 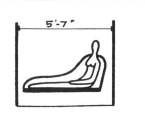

Nino's first diagram shows the space required for sitting upright, a posture still occasionally assumed in the living room of today.

Relaxed posture and low modern chairs imply that more space will be needed for chair and sitter—almost twice the upright sitter's.

Tall men, in what is often their favorite chair—a Saarinen relaxation chair or a Morris chair in low gear—stretch out to more than 6'-6".

A lady who wants to emulate Mme. Recamier in a chaise longue, requires a space 5'-7" long. Minimum width is still 2'-4".

   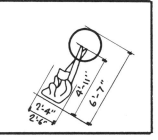

If you want to seat people in a sofa in front of a fine view seen through a large window facing south, study this diagram.

Adequate headroom must be provided when you want to open the living room on to a terrace or balcony, however small it may be.

Repetto has seated two people at a corner lamp table. One is in a lower, deeper seat than the other, but the lamp is adequate for both.

The leg room and shoulder room required in order to spend a quiet evening at home with a book is more ample than most of us realize.

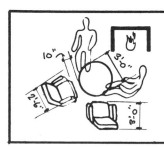 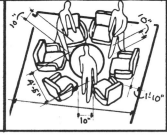 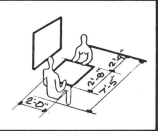 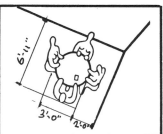

Seated around a small table, in comfortable chairs, within the right distance from the fire, a congenial conversation group.

A circle of arm chairs around a small table makes an ideal conversation group. Leg room, passage room, and chair room are indicated here.

Dining corner for two, in the kind of living room that is also a one room apartment. Window is at a good height for light and view.

To play a hand of bridge or have a snack at a round table in a corner of the living room requires the space indicated in this drawing.

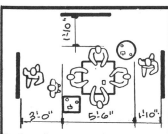 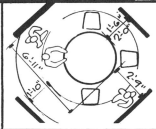 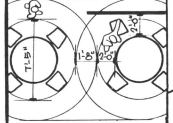 

You can play cards, or serve an informal meal, in an alcove 10'-6" long. One side must provide passage space for two which is 3 feet.

The minimum space required for a dining alcove with a round table is indicated here. Extra passage space is always needed at one wall.

The lesson implied by this diagram is that if you want to use two or more small tables together, round ones require less space than square.

Those who would place a long coffee table in front of a sofa, often under-estimate the depth required from back of sofa to coffee table edge.

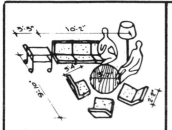 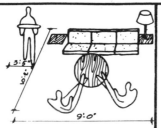 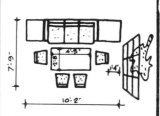 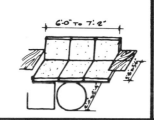

Here again, a group of furnishings which require more space than we are apt to realize; the pieces, however, have been scaled down in size.

A tried and true living room furniture arrangement. Guests face one another and the waiter (or anyone else entering the room).

You always have some kind of a table near the sofa. This drawing gives the dimensions of a medium-sized sofa and a choice of tables.

Good arrangement for a sofa and companion chairs near window. Light, knee room, and conversation angle are adequate for everyone.

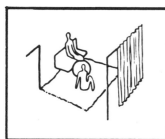  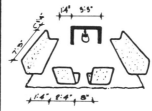 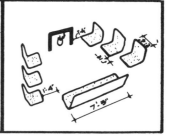

Nino suggests here a pleasant arrangement for a minimal sitting corner in one of those minimal modern living-dining rooms.

Compare this drawing with the one on the left and see why you shouldn't place a seating unit with a table before it, beside a door.

A fireplace grouping that has remained deservedly popular for a long period. This arrangement requires a loft-sized living room.

A variant of the symmetrical fireplace grouping at the left. Steam, radiant, hot air, and atomic heat have not yet ousted the fireplace.

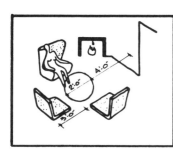 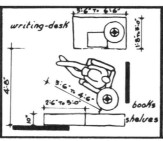 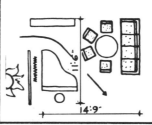 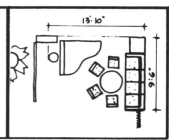

Three chairs in a conversation group, at the right distance from a corner fireplace. Fire can be tended without disturbing sitters.

Lazy man's relaxation corner. It is interesting to note that everything is built in except the chair. Refrigerator and bar could be added.

The pianist at the Baby Grand gets the best of the sunlight in this suggested arrangement. His audience is well placed for seeing and hearing.

Another good arrangement for a room with a piano, assuring again that the pianist has good light and that the audience can see and hear.

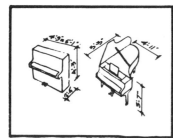 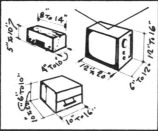 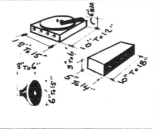 

Nino reminds the musically minded that the piano is a space-hog. The upright takes up less floor space but its height is a visual problem.

Radio and tv portables and consoles come in a variety of sizes and proportions but these are typical among commercial makes.

Hi fi, stereo, and tape recorders have changed the shape of record-playing equipment and storage (p. 65). Some typical units.

The distracted Turkish rug weaver who has just found a burning cigarette in the rug is accompanied by some standard rug sizes.

THE DINING ROOM

No interior is as important as the human interior, so in devoting this space to the proper arrangements of dining rooms we feel we are performing a double service. Man, that consuming animal, needs space to eat, but he doesn't need as much space for the purpose as he does to discourse or to play games.

The introductory drawing shows two of the most common faults in dining room design. Either tables are so crowded that elbows and fish forks threaten to become lethal weapons, or else people are placed so far apart that they need some sort of visual signal like wigwagging, in order to exchange ideas on the state of the soup.

The illustration at right shows the minimum space needed for eight people to dine in comfort. These measurements are amplified and broken down so you will notice that although 3'-4" is all the passageway that Hilda needs to pass the fish, there must be at least 4'-4" of floor space beyond the end of the table if she is to avoid conking the master with the swinging door.

Man cannot live without food; man cannot approach civilization until he has learned to consume his food with dignity; and so the most important piece of furniture in man's physical and spiritual life is a table. We say spiritual advisedly, because the sacrament behind all religions is the act of dining. Sacrifices, burned or living, are a dinner for the gods. Communion and the Mass, the fundamental sacrament of Christianity, are the Lord's dinner that we share. Christian or pagan, some kind of God's table is essential.

One of the immediate problems then, for us weak mortals, is the dining table and also the chairs and other appurtenances that belong to it. At right, below, a diagram illustrating the measurements necessary for a formal dining room in which eight people can eat in comfort and grace.

All the instruments and devices that civilized man needs to finish a meal occupy a rectangle approximately 24" x 15" though the standard table mat, now rapidly supplanting the table cloth, is 18 inches wide. A number of ladies have built careers teaching the timid how to arrange these implements. Basic rule: start at the outside and eat in.

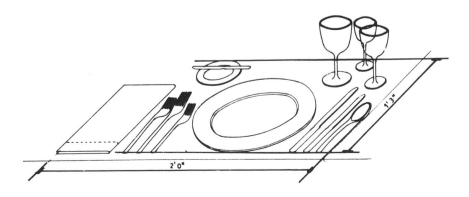

2'0"

1'3"

Two feet per person is a safe rule in estimating the seating capacity of a table, but if the head of the house is accustomed to carving and serving he is going to need considerable elbow space as explained above. For correct proportions of tables in general turn to the next page.

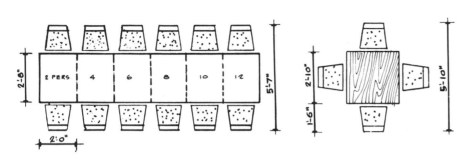

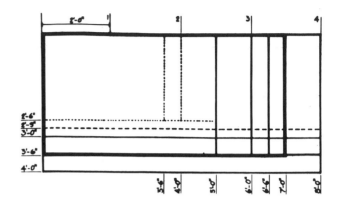

How to seat four at a square table (above); how to expand it lengthwise only and how to expand length and width proportionately.

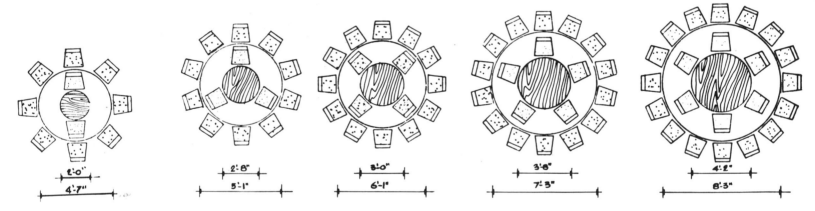

To approximate the size of round table needed to seat a given number of people, multiply number of people by width of place setting (2'-2" for armless, 2'-4" for armchairs) and divide the result by 3.14. The enlargement of round and oval tables is diagrammed at right. Width of each leaf should equal one place setting—2'-2" for armless, 2'-4" for arm chairs.

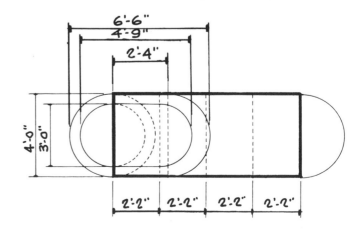

The dimensions of the dining table and the simpler variations of room arrangements which are dependent on the dimensions of the table and on the space requirements for the movement of chairs, diners, and servants are of prime importance.

The drawings on the opposite page demonstrate the seating capacities of various size tables—square, rectangular, round, and oval and how the size (and therefore the floor space) of any given table must be expanded in order to accommodate additional diners in comfort. The average allotment of space per diner allowed by dining table manufacturers is 2 feet but 2'-2" is preferred and 2'-4" should be considered the civilized minimum where arm chairs are employed. For rectangular tables additional space must be allowed at the head and the foot of the table—4 inches to 8 inches more. The range in widths of the rectangular table is from 1'10"to 3'-7".

Diagrams overleaf show how to place the different sizes and shapes of tables in the separate dining room.

In the course of working out these plans, it may be well to remind the reader of certain simple considerations that should not be forgotten while the job is in progress: to concentrate the lighting at the top of the tables and above the serving tables; to place outlets for the bell within arm reach near the table on the wall or within foot reach on the floor; and to place outlets for the server and the warmer near the serving table.

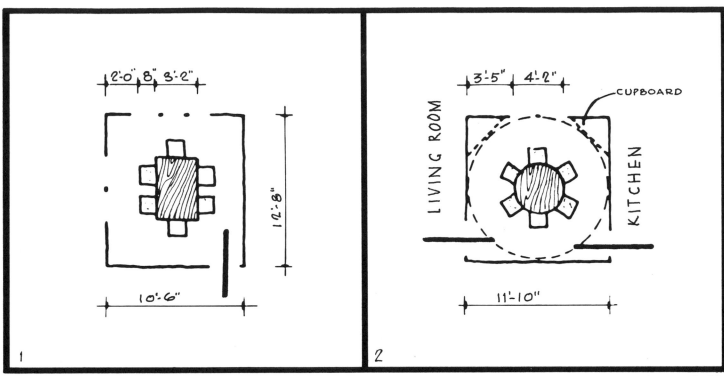

1

2

Minimal dining room. This arrangement is for a rectangular table in a rectangular room and there are no cupboards or additional furniture.

At last, we reach the size room which can hold all the furniture that used to be considered standard equipment.

Minimal rectangular dining room, this time with a round table and corner cupboards.

Repetto suggests a symmetrical layout for a living-dining room. Dining area is partitioned from living area, and the table is smack in the middle of the dining area.

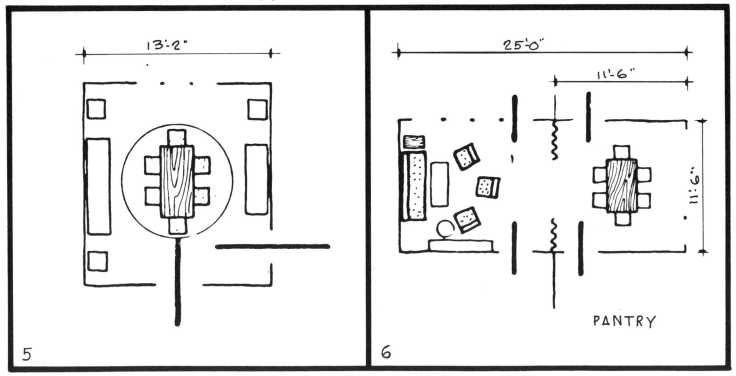

5

6

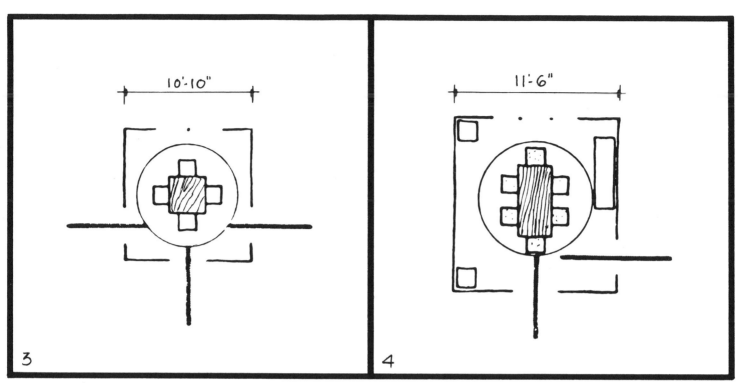

3

4

You can't get a separate dining room smaller than this one, which holds no extra furniture at all.

The separate dining room, this time with room for six plus two extra chairs and a commode.

Living-dining room treated as an integrated unit, with the table in a corner.

A more complicated asymmetrical layout for the living-dining room based on careful analysis of traffic lines and of the use of space.

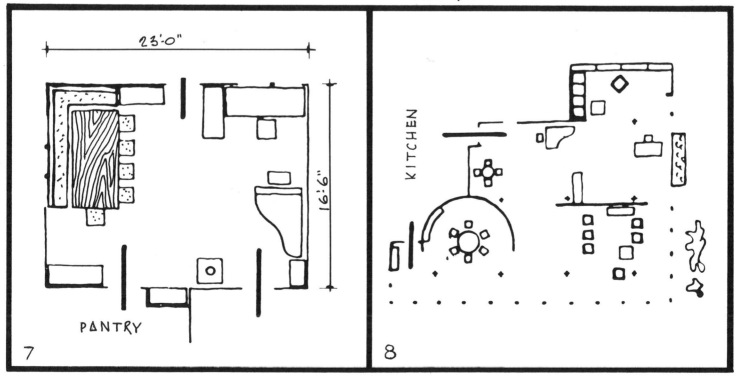

7

8

We have for many reasons always been in favor of a revival of the separate dining room, or at least a dining space that insures privacy. It is the years and years of looking at garbage that gives sanitation inspectors their world-weary expression, and we believe that removing as many people as possible from the presence of dirty dishes is one of the great functions of architecture. It must be admitted, however, that the fact that this dining area is generally used but three times a day is the principal reason why builders eager to save space try to make people eat either in the living room or in the kitchen.

It is possible to blame the whole thing on humany anatomy and the habits of western civilization. People haven't got enough joints, and they atrophy those that they have. If all infants were taught to squat, to sit crosslegged on the ground, and to eat delicately with their fingers as in most of Africa, Melanesia, and Japan, we could save considerable storage and dining space, but unfortunately this has not happened. We need not only tables, but chairs, plates, forks, etc. and they take up room. The only President who could have been comfortable squatting on the White House floor was Andrew Johnson, because he was trained as a tailor and made his own inaugural frock coat.

However, be that as it may, the so-called living-dining area is with us and the drawings opposite indicate three possible arrangements of same, including measurements.

In the relationship between the kitchen and dining room an open plan quite often provides for shelves or storage units that double as a visual barrier between the two areas. Such an arrangement can be extremely convenient, particularly if it includes a "pass-through" or serving window. One drawing opposite also indicates some of the dimensional considerations involved.

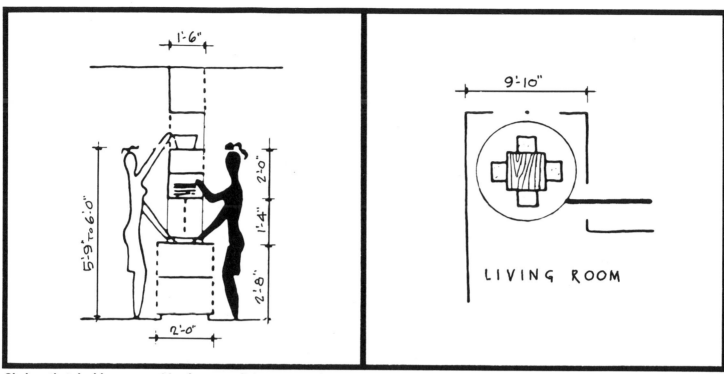

Shelves that double as a partition between dining room and kitchen or pantry are extremely convenient, particularly if they include a pass-through. Here are proper heights for shelves and counter.

Here the width is the same as the room at right above but slightly more length is required.

This and the following two sketches show ways to arrange a living-room alcove for dining.

This final drawing assumes the same size table as the one at left pushed against the wall. This leaves part of the space for other uses except when more seating is required at table.

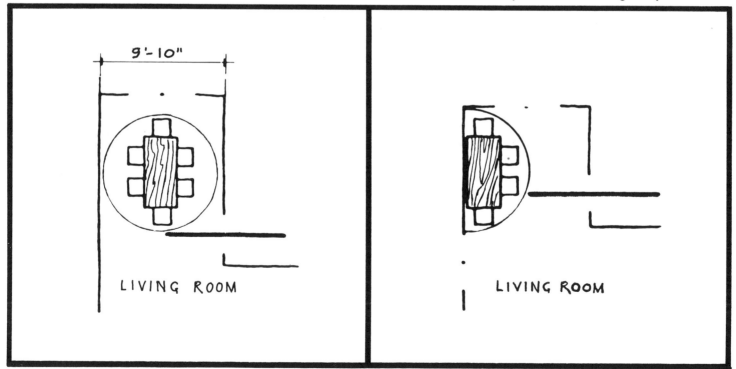

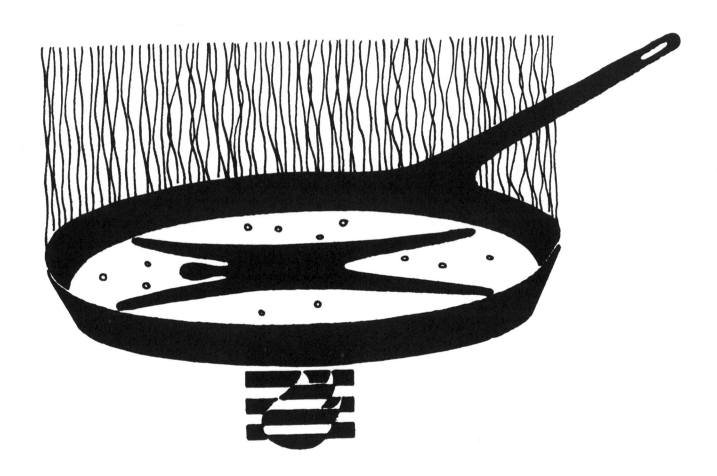

THE KITCHEN

The kitchen has undergone perhaps more transformation within the last half century than any other room in the American home. In the pre-central heating days the warmth of its coal or wood-burning range made it as much a place for entertaining friends as a culinary laboratory over which grandmother reigned supreme. Moreover, its size, by today's standards, was enormous and served as quantitative proof of its relative importance.

With the passing of time the perfection of gadgets, and the invention of the push-button, the kitchen was somewhat reduced in size and became more utilitarian in function than social. It is, naturally, within this more contemporary frame of reference that we shall try to outline some of the basic design considerations.

In the diagrams overleaf we have attempted to illustrate not only the general areas of kitchen activity but the over-all dimensional requirements involved as well.

THE BASIC ACTIVITIES

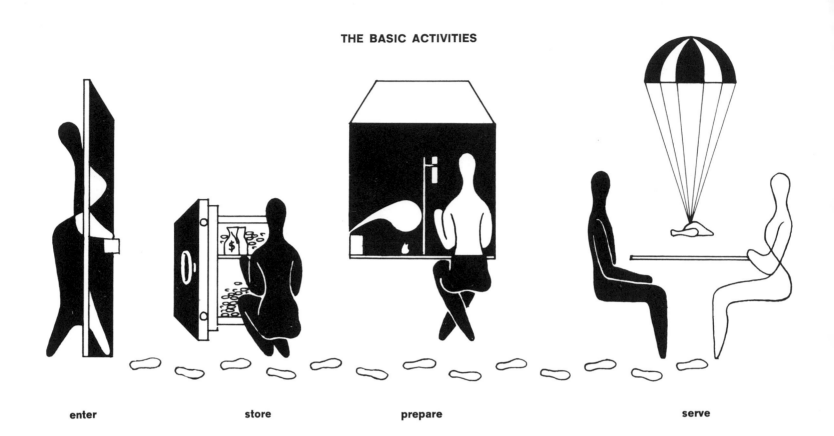

enter   **store**   **prepare**   **serve**

ARRANGEMENTS

AVERAGE WIDTH
24" TO 26"
RANGE TO 30"

4'-0"

8'-8" TO 9'-0"

14'-6" TO 18'-6"

10'-0" TO 12'-0"

4'-0"

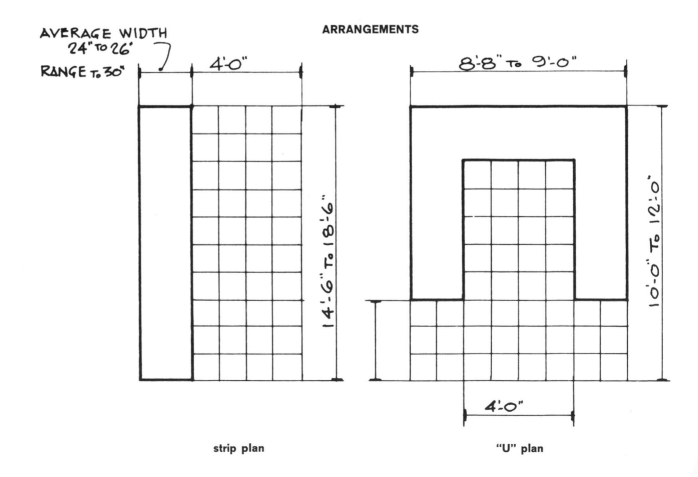

strip plan   **"U" plan**

THE WORK GROUP

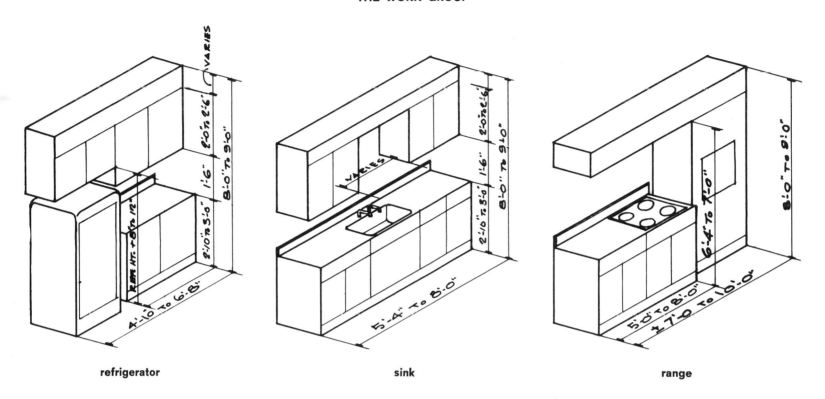

refrigerator   **sink**   **range**

ARRANGEMENTS

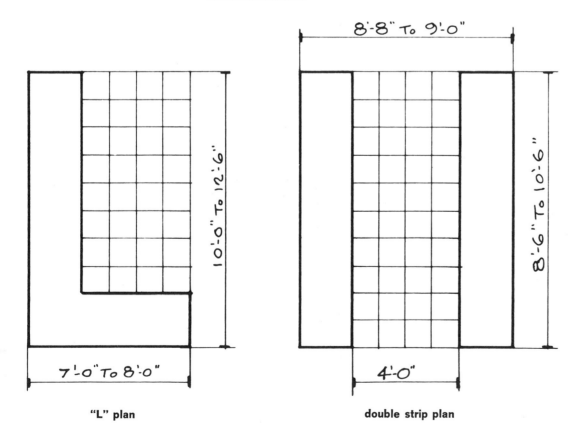

"L" plan   **double strip plan**

In the following diagrams, however, these dimensional requirements are broken down to include, among other little gems, the height of the highest cabinet shelf for comfortable access by those members of the human race having normal glandular conditions and measurements of most standard kitchen equipment from wall ovens to dripping faucets. Conspicuous in its absence is any greatly detailed gossip relative to storage of kitchen items: this topic will be dealt with separately in a later section on storage.

For good measure (no pun intended) and as a warning to those of you who are tempted to ignore our pearls of wisdom, we have also thrown in several good examples of bad design.

Arrangement below, left, in terms of refrigerator location and door swings, is great for fraternity initiations, tired blood, and flabby muscles, but as an ideal for efficient kitchen planning fails lamentably. Location of the highest shelf as shown below, center, works rather well for Watusi tribesmen and Tibetan balancing teams but, unfortunately, all it can afford the average couple is an increased sense of "togetherness." At right, below, although inadequate clearance between cabinets can provide momentary comfort while tending the range, it limits use of kitchen equipment to tall thin people.

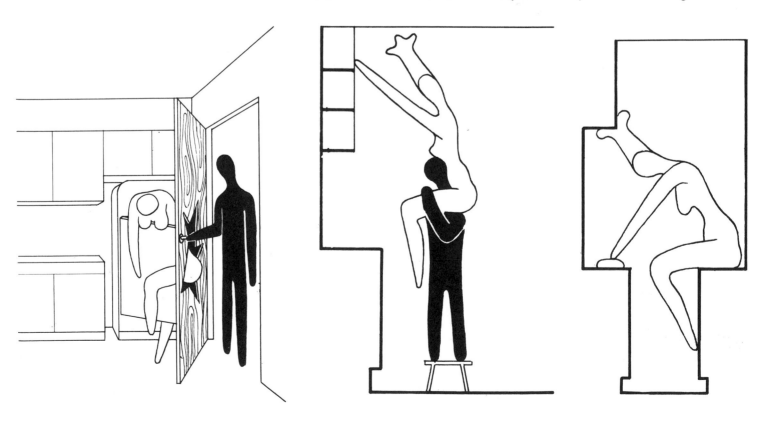

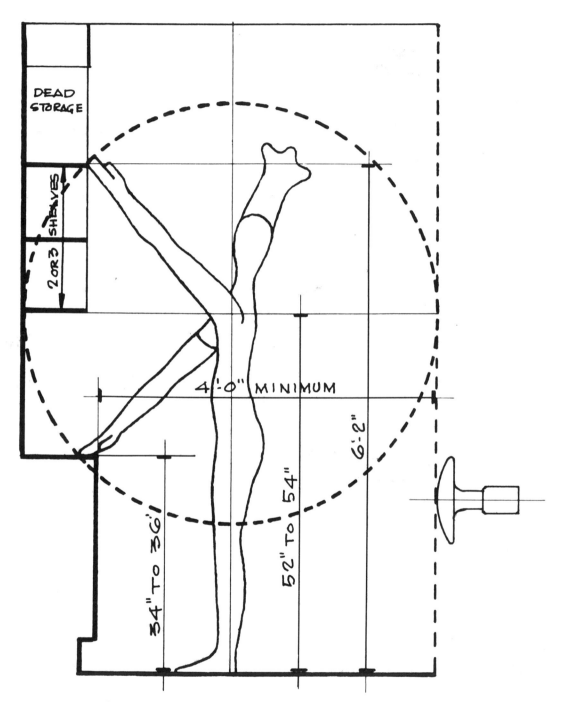

DEAD STORAGE

SHELVES

2 OR 3

4'-0" MINIMUM

6'-2"

54" TO 36"

52" TO 54"

Some of the minimum measurements essential to good design.

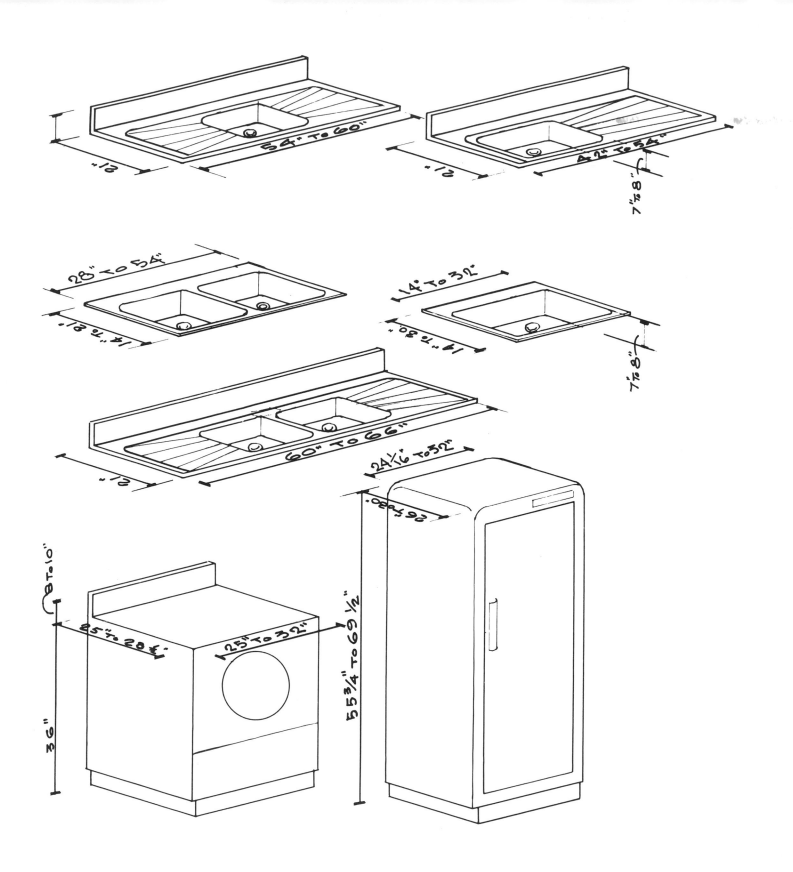

These drawings show the range of basic sizes for such common kitchen equipment as refrigerators, ranges, sinks, dish washers, and wall ovens.

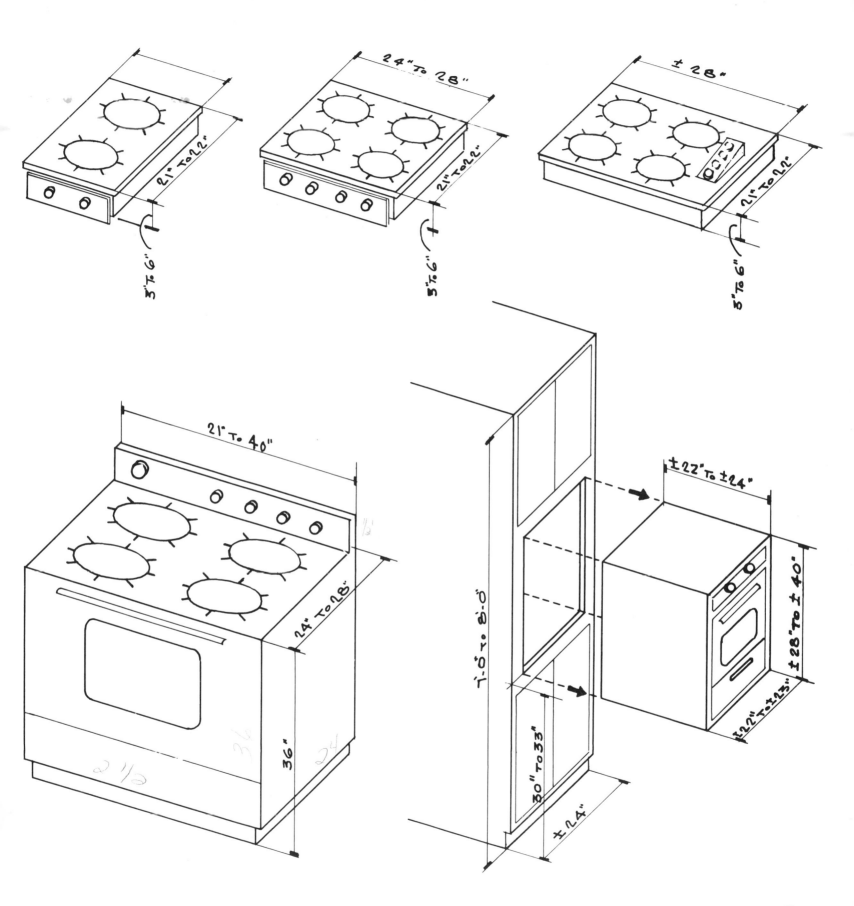

24" To 28"

± 28"

21" To 22"

21" To 22"

21" To 22"

3" To 6"

3" To 6"

3" To 6"

21" To 40"

24" To 28"

36"

± 22" To ± 24"

7'-0" To 8'-0"

± 28" To ± 40"

± 22" To ± 23"

30" To 33"

± 24"

THE BEDROOM

"In bed we laugh, in bed we cry
And born in bed, in bed we die"

These touching words were written in the seventeenth century by Issac De Benserade, a French poet of the time. We quote him for no other purpose than to establish the fact that our preoccupation with the bedroom is by no means singular nor even necessarily Freudian. As a matter of fact, Napoleon himself admitted that bed had become such a luxury to him he would not exchange it for all the thrones of the world. Moreover, since statistics indicate that man spends one third of his lifetime sleeping, we feel a case for the bedroom has been well made.

Having thus established the importance of this little chamber, it would be reasonable to devote the next few pages to some of the planning problems involved.

Nino's drawings show some of the basic minimum clearances between furniture elements and the average range of sizes for common bedroom furniture.

The drawings overleaf indicate two of the most common faults in bedroom planning.

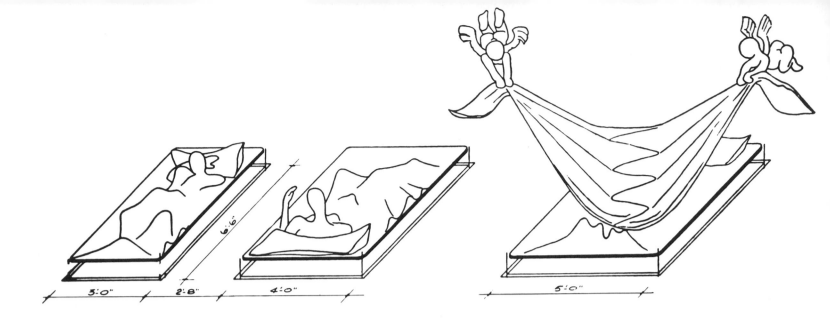

The 3-foot cot is the narrowest couch that train, plane, or space capsule has any right to put a person in. The beckoning lady lies in a three-quarter bed. Most manufacturers consider 54 inches standard for double beds. Five feet is better.

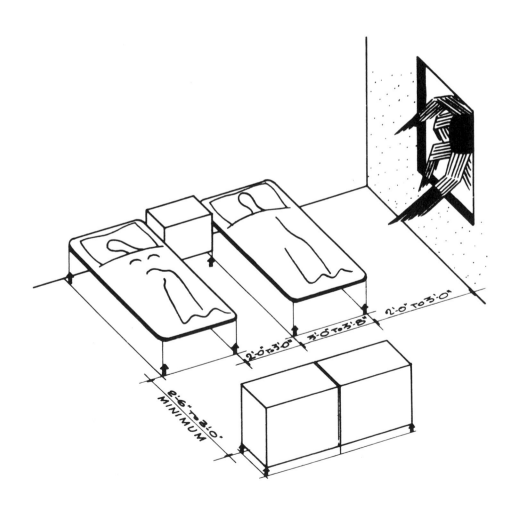

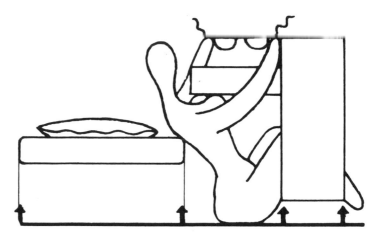

A corner located bed may prove to be a great back-breaking space-saver since it requires vertical as well as lateral movement in order to be made.

Inadequate clearance between bed and dresser may cause nostalgia in a retired contortionist but bruises are the only likely result for anyone else.

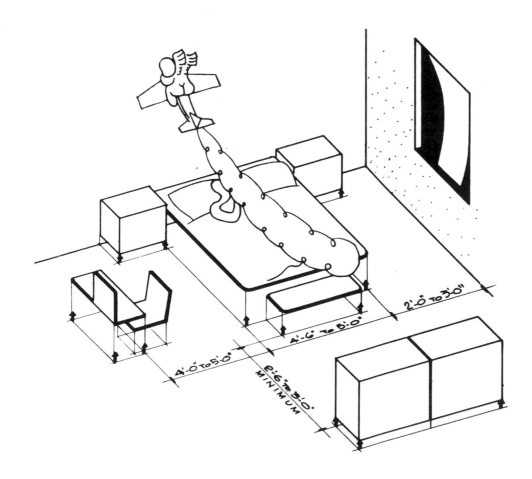

2'-0" to 3'-0"

4'-0" to 5'-0"

4'-0" to 5'-0"

2'-6" to 3'-0" MINIMUM

THE FAMILY ROOM

It is generally accepted that in addition to acute alcoholism, narcotic addiction, and navel contemplation, there is yet a fourth dimension to family relaxation—namely the family room, alias game room, multipurpose room, "rec" room, and what-have-you.

In the design of such areas measurements and proportions are vital. On the following pages you will find the proper shapes and proportions for card tables, and pool tables, and ping-pong tables, movie projectors, dart boards, punching bags, and shuffle boards, but more important than that, you will find the amount of anatomical space needed for human beings to operate these devices and play these games comfortably and (we hope) with some success.

Twenty feet from projector screen gives the largest and brightest image for most home movie projectors. Since the distance from the eyes to the top of the head is approximately 4 inches, arrange seats progressively 5 inches lower, to give unobstructed viewing. A side angle of more than 30° from the plane of the screen gives distortion.

Folding card furniture, and the space it occupies. Poker tables are round, for poker may be played by an odd number of people, not counting kibitzers.

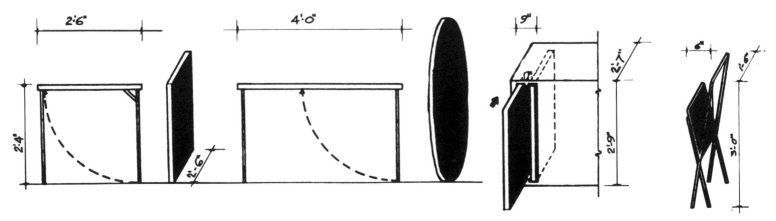

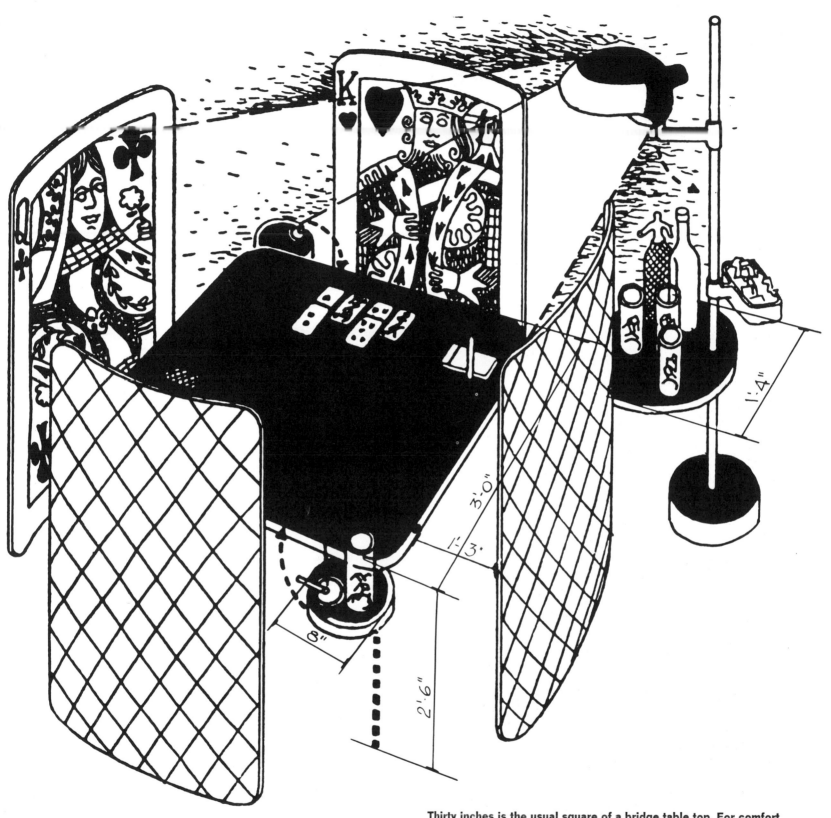

Thirty inches is the usual square of a bridge table top. For comfort we suggest a 36-inch semi-permanent table with pivoting corner trays for drinks and smokes. A bridge table and four players occupy 5 square feet of floor space. Allow minimum 18 inches passageway between tables. Note special lamp with holder for ice cube tray and shade casting light on table only.

The Kelly pool player who hast just torn the cloth and wishes he could vanish is used to illustrate the size billiard table found in those homes that have them. A 12'-0" x 6'-8½" tournament table is not only too large but might easily crash through the floor since it weighs approximately one ton. Allow 5 feet of space all the way around the table to avoid poking side-liners in the eye.

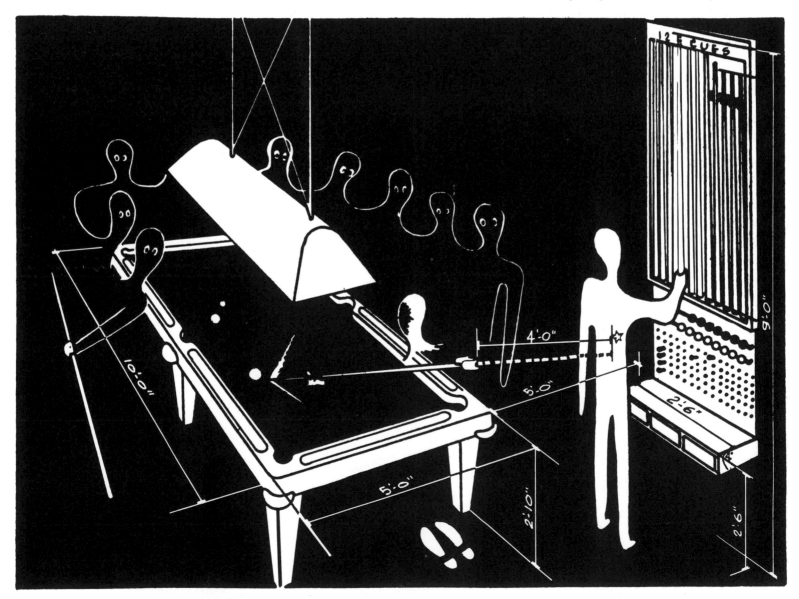

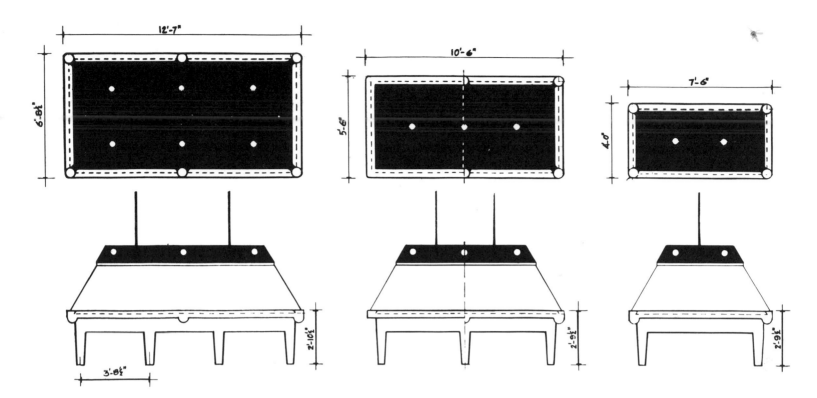

Even many habitués of pool rooms are unaware that billiard tables come in seven standard sizes. The drawings above illustrate the three most popular, together with the correct lighting for each. The 4' x 7' junior billiard table above at right is particularly popular in homes and in summer camp recreation rooms.

It is possible to play ping-pong with some comfort with about 7 feet of runback beyond the table ends, and 5 feet on either side. Experts prefer 12 feet of runback. This is a tournament table. Folding tables are smaller.

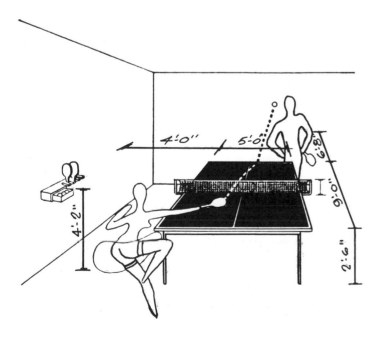

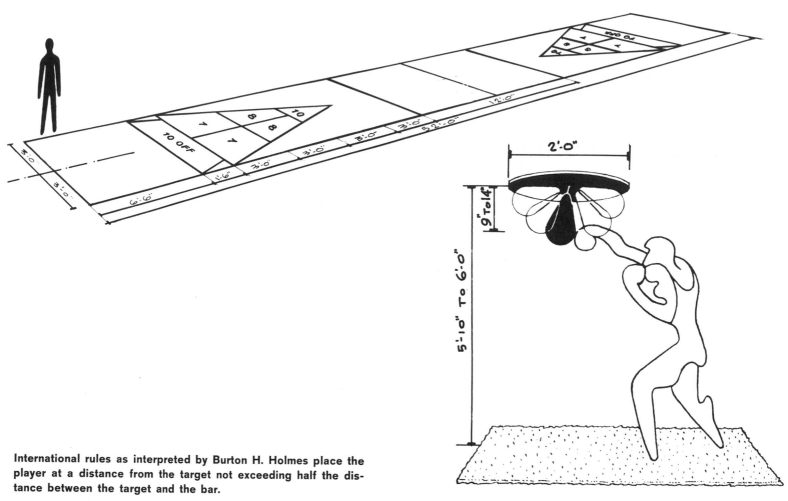

International rules as interpreted by Burton H. Holmes place the player at a distance from the target not exceeding half the distance between the target and the bar.

The drawings opposite round out our section on the game room by giving data relative to several other recreational pastimes, from dart throwing to bag punching. For less energetic readers the final drawing gives the latest low-down on yo-yo measurements. Please note we have indicated only the junior type yo-yo. Also on the market is an "executive" yo-yo—which comes in an oiled walnut finish. So vast is the range of sizes it is beyond the scope of this book to indicate them all. We did, however, establish a very definite relationship between YYD (Avenue jargon for yo-yo diameter) and E.S. (Executive status). All data seems to indicate that the bigger the wheel the bigger the diameter but as of this writing we have been unable to translate this into any kind of equation.

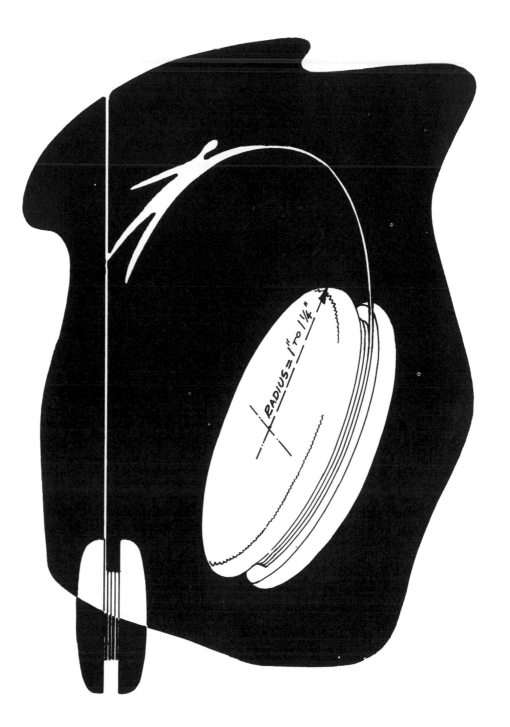

STORAGE SPACE

Just prior to the publication of this third edition of Anatomy we were advised of a certain archaeological find of great significance to our ensuing discussion about storage facilities. Recent excavations have unearthed two excellent examples of the early closetoria, forerunner of the contemporary closet. The on-site sketches (across) of the ancient facilities show some of the basic nomenclature involved.

Essentially the closetorium consisted of two vertical slabs of stone supporting a third, horizontal, slab. A hole was drilled at each side slab through which was inserted a sturdy cypress branch called the "clothesum rodumus." It is most interesting to note the difference in size of the two structures found. Observe that the closetorium shown at the left is much smaller. Notice also that this amazingly well preserved find has but one fig leaf hanging from the rodumus while the other closetorium has three. Deducing that the latter belonged to a female ancestress we might point out its significance: it demonstrates that, historically, at least, if not anatomically, the female has always required more storage facilities.

So much for a look into the early origins of the storage problem. Let us now examine its development in contemporary terms.

The dozens of garments and accessories with which man is now accustomed to adorn himself must be measured carefully in order to stow them efficiently. To show the smallest space into which the wardrobe of a likely male client can be compressed we have designed a cabinet 5'-6" x 6'-4" x 2'-0" which will contain everything that the well-dressed man needs to wear. All designers should realize that these same measurements will help them just as much in designing closets, bureau drawers, wardrobe luggage, or packing cases.

Nobody should plan a bedroom, or a dormitory, or a locker room, or a chest of drawers, or a suitcase, without memorizing most of the proportions of the male impedimenta shown below and overleaf. The female equivalents, although much more compact, take up three times as much room as will be found by studying the counterparts to these on pages 58 and 59.

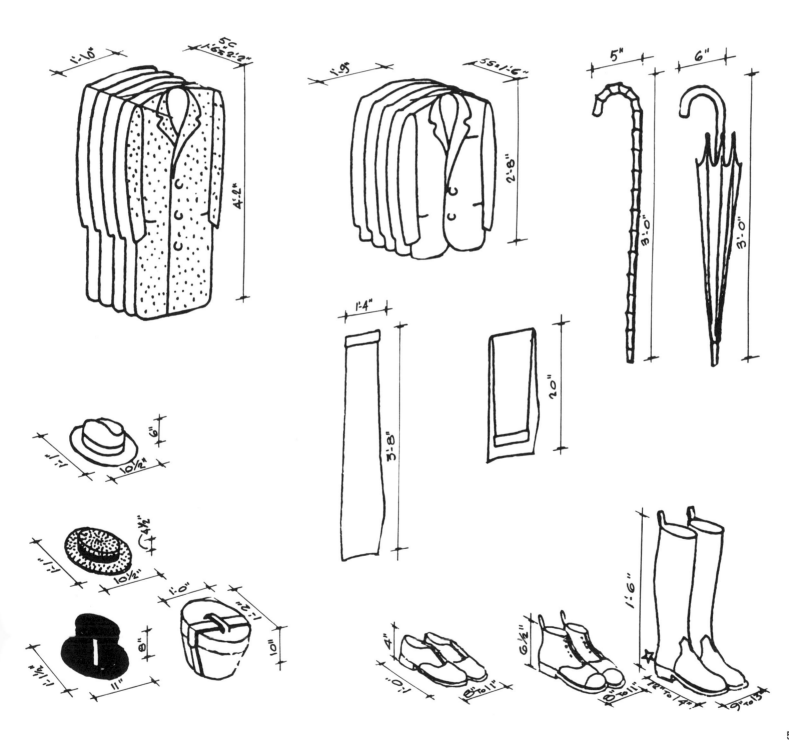

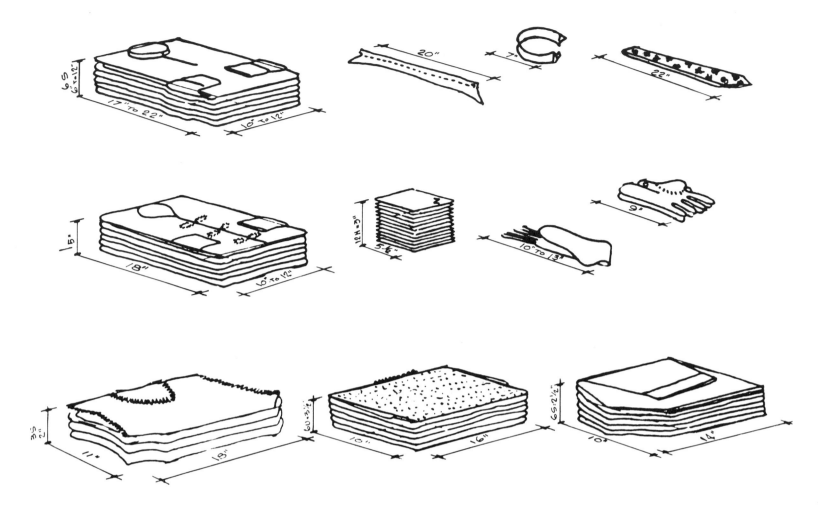

Strip a hall closet of its bare essentials and bring it out in the open and you have the corner arrangement shown at left. Note the decorative circular coat hangers. There are many reasons why a coat closet should be 24 inches deep, but the most obvious one is that a man's shoulders are 18 inches wide, and hangers need breathing space.

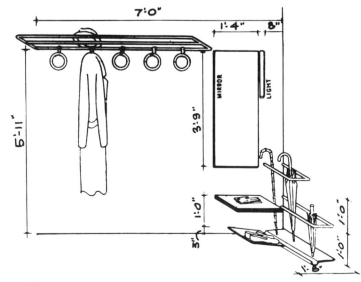

Everything that the average man needs to keep his chin up in the presence of Marlon Brando, Yves Montand, or Elvis Presley can be stowed, and not compressed, in the wardrobe below. Furniture designers please note that three shirts in one bureau drawer are enough. Three drawers for "little affairs" may be too many.

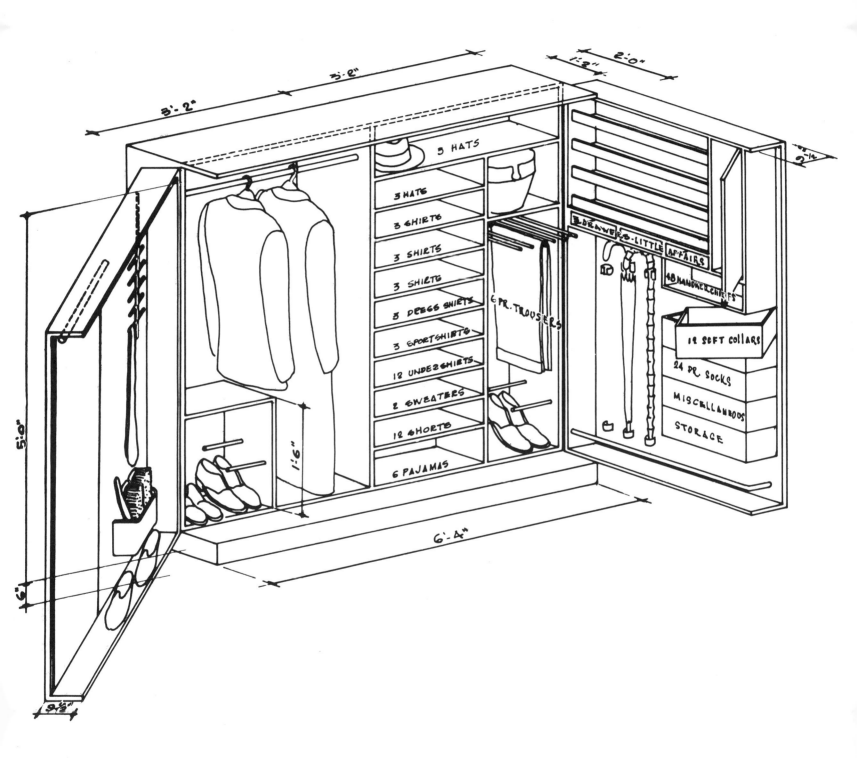

To show how compactly all the clothing needed to cover the average man's anatomy for a whole season could be stowed, our artist was able to design a single cabinet, 6'-4" long x 2' deep. Yet though the most painstaking research, checked and rechecked, proved that all that average young woman wears at any one time weighs just 1 lb. 11 ozs., and though the wardrobe chosen has been selected and approved by the editors of Brides Magazine, it has proven impossible to compress it into anything less than three cabinets, each 3'-9" long x 6'-6" x 2' deep. Most of the young women we know have far less storage space. Frankly, we don't see how they do it.

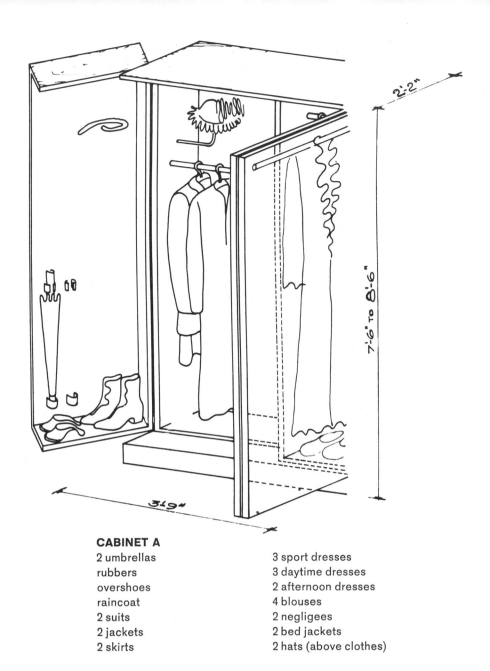

CABINET A

2 umbrellas	3 sport dresses
rubbers	3 daytime dresses
overshoes	2 afternoon dresses
raincoat	4 blouses
2 suits	2 negligees
2 jackets	2 bed jackets
2 skirts	2 hats (above clothes)

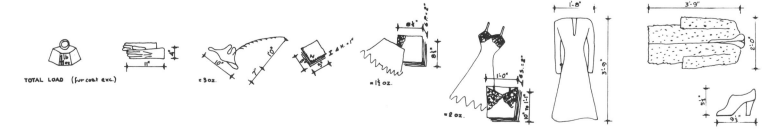

TOTAL LOAD (fur coat exc.)

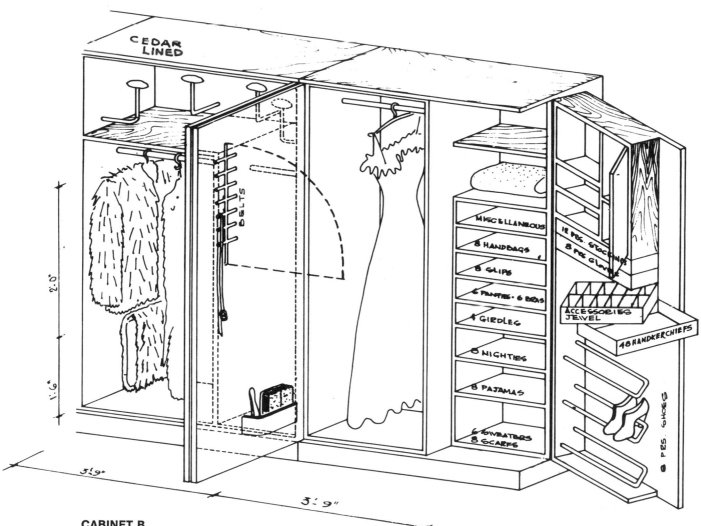

Labels in drawing: CEDAR LINED · BELTS · MISCELLANEOUS · 8 HANDBAGS · 8 SLIPS · 6 PANTIES · 6 BRAS · 4 GIRDLES · 8 NIGHTIES · 8 PAJAMAS · 6 SWEATERS · 8 SCARFS · 12 PRS. STOCKINGS · 8 PRS. GLOVES · ACCESSORIES JEWEL · 48 HANDKERCHIEFS · 8 PRS. SHOES · 3'-0" · 6'-1" · 3'-9" · 3'-9"

CABINET B

mules—slippers
1 fur muff
1 fur jacket or short cape
1 fur piece
2 fur coats
3 coats
4 hats (above clothes)

CABINET C

belts
2 brushes
2 dinner dresses
2 evening dresses
1 evening wrap
2 housecoats
storage (as indicated)

These three cabinets are more than a guide for architects, cabinet makers, luggage builders, and others interested in designing storage space. They have been planned to accommodate a complete wardrobe for the average American girl. It seems like a lot. In the drawing these units are geared to formal and winter wear. In warm weather heavy coats, winter dresses, and sweaters give way to toreador pants, short shorts, bikinis, beach robes, and damp towels.

The human stomach is a most useful organ, shaped like the working part of a bagpipe (not unnaturally, since bagpipe bags were originally made from cows', sheep's, and goats' stomachs). Normally the human stomach contains a little more than a quart. The equipment needed to keep that bag comfortably and elegantly filled has called forth the efforts of architects, interior designers, furniture designers, weavers, potters, glass blowers, silversmiths, and the predecessors of Emily Post (not to mention cooks) for century after century.

Besides his eager fingers and his bare teeth, the first essential implement for dining that primitive man needed was a spoon. It was a hollowed sliver of wood if he lived in the Scandinavian or other northern countries, and a sea shell if he lived on the shore of the Mediterranean or other seas, but it was essential, because man has never yet learned how to eat soup with his fingers.

We have come a long way since then. And nowadays we must have storage for all manner of things, useful and useless, or go out of our minds. Among the measurements the designer will find on the following pages are sizes of phonograph records, individual and collective, tape for tape recorders, and proper vaults for storing same. You will also find correct measurements and suggested arrangements for more articles for eating and drinking than you or your clients are ever likely to use but for each of which you may occasionally have to make space in a sideboard or pantry.

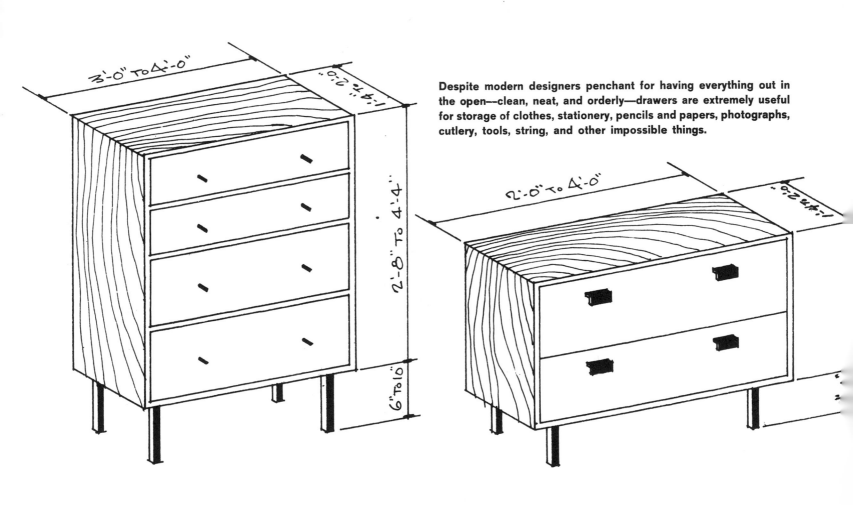

Despite modern designers penchant for having everything out in the open—clean, neat, and orderly—drawers are extremely useful for storage of clothes, stationery, pencils and papers, photographs, cutlery, tools, string, and other impossible things.

Another common storage problem is that of phonograph records. Since surrealist clients are few and far between, vertical storage is the best idea—it avoids that scrunchy bounce of the needle on the warped record. Of course, vertical storage calls for either lynx-eyes or an efficient library system and will continue to do so until the days of the fat (possibly rubber) record arrive.

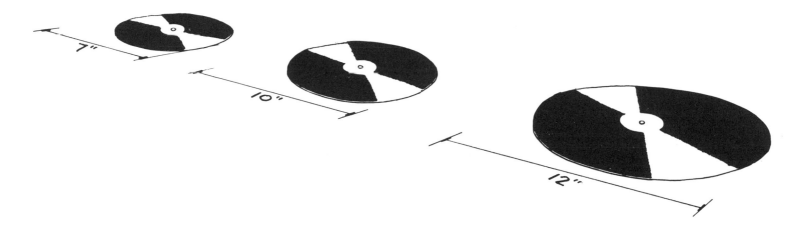

The drawing above indicates the diameters of standard records while below Nino shows how many records would be contained in a pile 1 foot high.

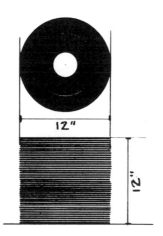

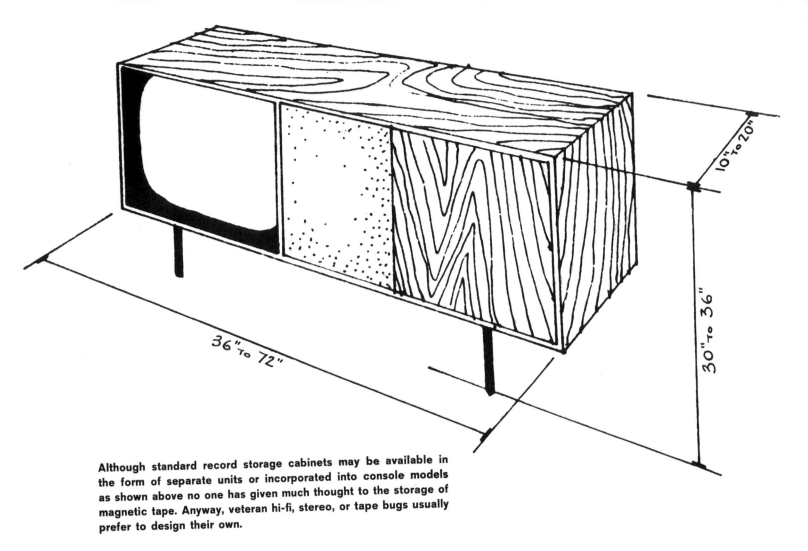

10" to 20"

30" to 36"

36" to 72"

Although standard record storage cabinets may be available in the form of separate units or incorporated into console models as shown above no one has given much thought to the storage of magnetic tape. Anyway, veteran hi-fi, stereo, or tape bugs usually prefer to design their own.

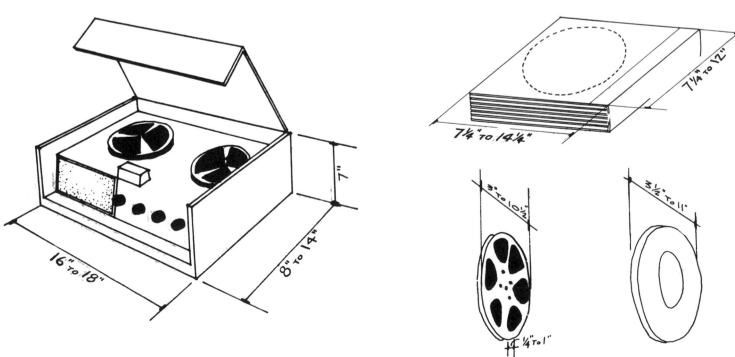

7"

16" to 18"

8" to 14"

7¼" to 12"

7¼" to 14¼"

3" to 10½"

3½" to 11"

¼" to 1"

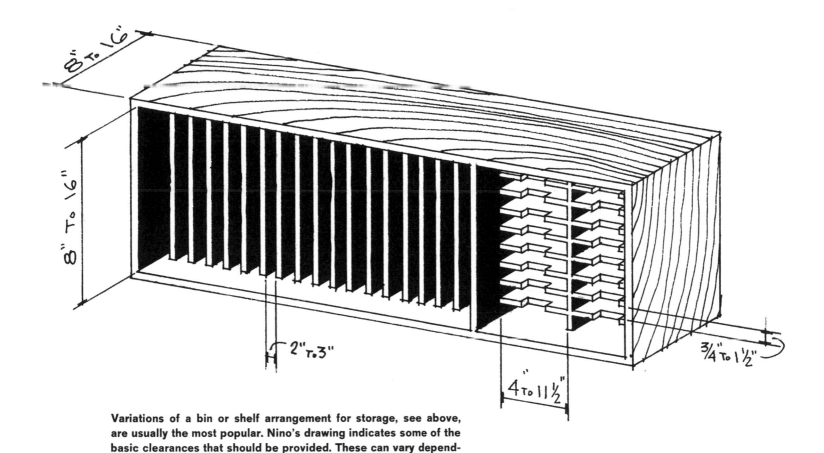

Variations of a bin or shelf arrangement for storage, see above, are usually the most popular. Nino's drawing indicates some of the basic clearances that should be provided. These can vary depending upon the size of the album or tape to be stored.

Approximate album sizes are shown at left while the size of tape containers may vary from 3½″ to 11″ in diameter or square as shown in the drawing. The actual tape reel itself is naturally slightly smaller and varies from about 3″ to 10½″ in diameter. Precaution: if you are building in tape storage keep it away from electrical outlets and switches or you may find your tape de-magnetized and blank when you want to run it.

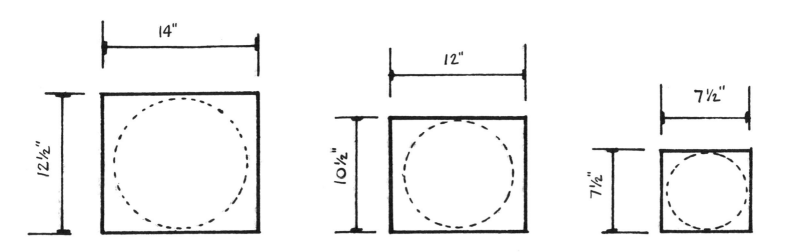

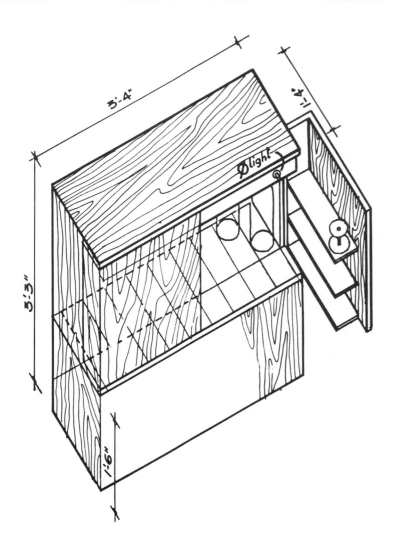

The piece of furniture at left could be a sideboard, or what used to be called a cellarette, a section of a public bar, or, should your liver desert you, a hi-fi or television cabinet.

For those of you who prefer your own bar, here are enough measurements for the most elaborate layout, but each measurement applies also to the simplest family room.

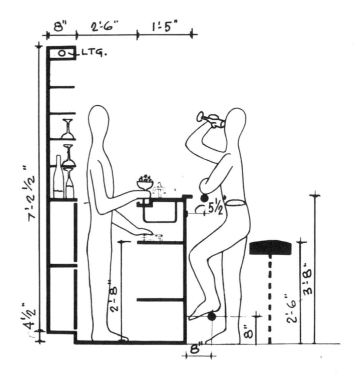

As in all sections of this book, the case work that we show is not to be thought of as an actual piece of furniture, but rather as an exemplar for a designer. It may be nice to know that if you have a client who needs six asparagus tongs, six egg cups, four hors d'oeuvre plates, two bottles of chianti, a corkscrew, and a nut cracker, you will be able to fit them in properly.

Overleaf we have listed the utensils required for a formal service for six and an informal service for four.

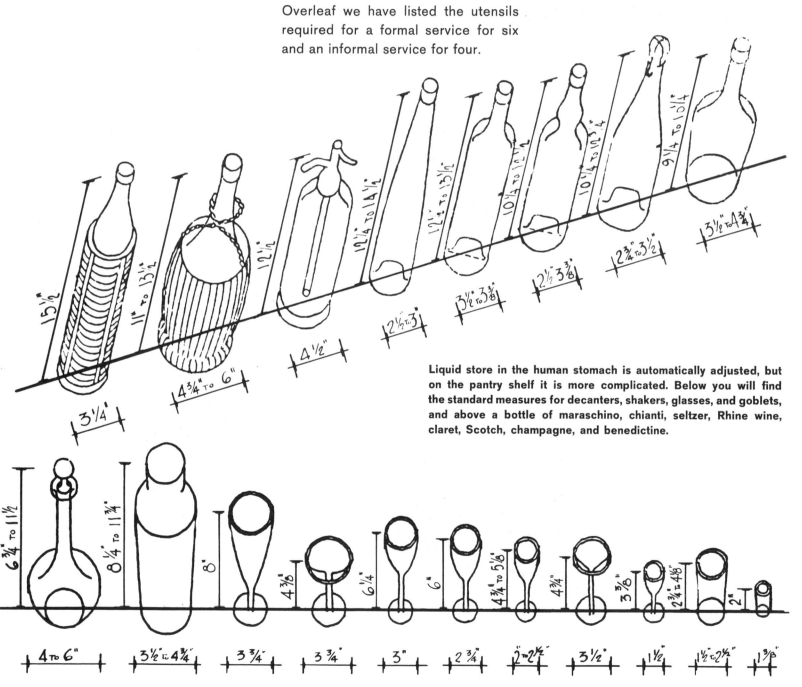

Liquid store in the human stomach is automatically adjusted, but on the pantry shelf it is more complicated. Below you will find the standard measures for decanters, shakers, glasses, and goblets, and above a bottle of maraschino, chianti, seltzer, Rhine wine, claret, Scotch, champagne, and benedictine.

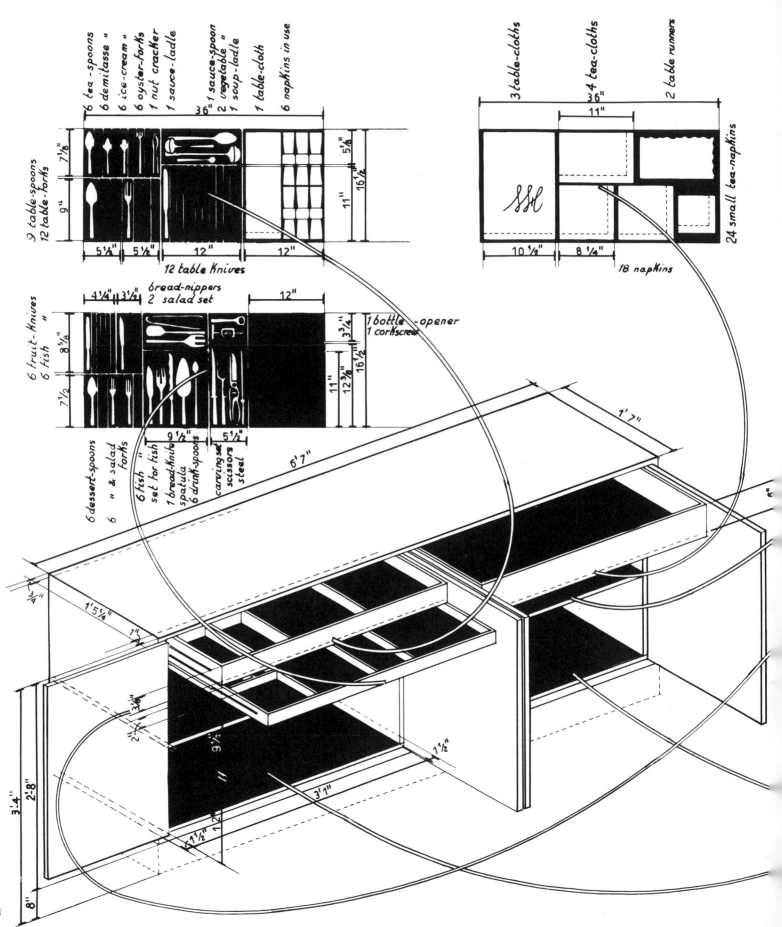

6 tea -spoons
6 demitasse "
6 ice-cream "
6 oyster-forks
1 nut cracker
1 sauce-ladle
36"
1 sauce-spoon
2 vegetable "
1 soup-ladle
1 table-cloth
6 napkins in use

7⅛"
9 table-spoons
12 table-forks
9"
5½" 5½" 12" 12"
5⅝"
16½"
11"

12 table Knives

6 fruit-Knives "
6 fish "
4¼" 3½"
bread-nippers
2 salad set
12"
8⅛"
7½"
3¾"
11" 12⅜" 16½"
1 bottle -opener
1 corkscrew

6 dessert-spoons
6 " & salad forks
6 fish "
set for fish
1 bread-knife
spatula
6 drink-spoons
carving set
scissors
steel
9½" 5½"

3 table-cloths
36"
11"
4 tea-cloths
2 table runners

SSL
24 small tea-napkins
10½" 8¼"
18 napkins

1' 7"
6"
6' 7"
1'5¼"
7"
3'-4"
2'-8"
¾"
2'1 3⅛"
9½"
11
7½"
3' 1"
6½" 1½" 12"
8"

68

Here Nino shows a sideboard holding a service for six. The reader can reduce the storage space needed for larger and smaller services. Correct height of the drawers is important, since many items are stacked. Grey dishes in the drawing are china; white are glass. Nino has allowed extra space for the numerous articles which may be de rigueur in certain social circles and certain countries but not in others.

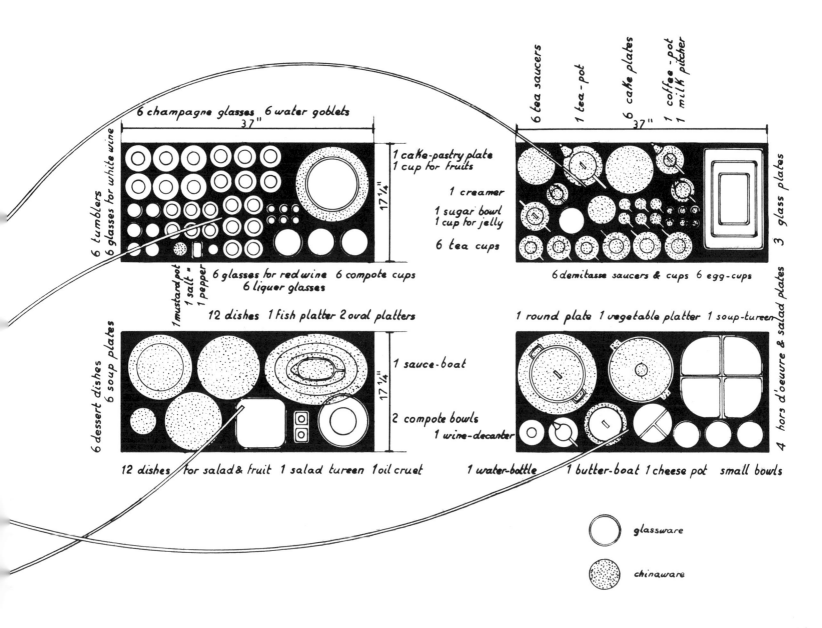

6 champagne glasses   6 water goblets
37"
17¼"

6 glasses for white wine
6 tumblers

1 cake-pastry plate
1 cup for fruits

1 creamer

1 sugar bowl
1 cup for jelly

6 tea cups

1 mustard pot
1 salt "
1 pepper

6 glasses for red wine   6 compote cups
6 liquer glasses

6 tea saucers   1 tea-pot   6 cake plates   1 coffee-pot
1 milk pitcher
37"

3 glass plates

6 demitasse saucers & cups   6 egg-cups

12 dishes   1 fish platter   2 oval platters

1 round plate   1 vegetable platter   1 soup-tureen

6 dessert dishes
6 soup plates

1 sauce-boat
17¼"

2 compote bowls
1 wine-decanter

12 dishes   for salad & fruit   1 salad tureen   1 oil cruet

4 hors d'oeuvre & salad plates

1 water-bottle   1 butter-boat   1 cheese pot   small bowls

glassware

chinaware

69

FORMAL SERVICE FOR 6

FLATWARE

9 tablespoons (3 for serving)	8¼″ x 1-9/16″
12 table forks	8¼″ x 13/16″
12 table knives	9-7/16″ x 1″
6 fish forks	7¼″ x 1″
6 fish knives	9-1/16″ x 1″
6 dessert spoons	7¼″ x 1-3/16″
6 dessert forks	5-15/16″ x 13/16″
6 fruit knives	7⅛″ x 11/16″
6 butter knives	6¾″ x 1-3/16″
6 oyster forks	6-5/16″ x 13/16″
6 egg spoons	4¾″ x 1-3/16″
6 teaspoons	6-5/16″ x 1⅛″
6 ice cream spoons	5½″ x 1-3/16″
6 demi-tasse spoons	4¾″ x 13/16″
6 tall drink spoons	9¼″ x 1″
6 pairs small asparagus tongs	5½″ x 1-3/16″
1 soup ladle	11-13/16″ x 2¾″
1 sauce ladle	7⅛″ x 2¾″
2 large spoons	10¼″ x 2-3/16″
1 carving set: knife	11¾″ x 1-3/16″
fork	11½″ x ⅞″
1 pair chicken scissors	10-11/16″ x 1¾″
2 meat forks	9⅞″ x 13/16″
1 fish set: knife	10⅝″ x 2″
fork	9-1/16″ x 2⅜″
1 salad set: spoon	8⅞″ x 1¾″
fork	8⅞″ x 1¾″
1 butter-cheese spatula	7⅛″ x 1-3/16″
1 bread knife	9⅞″ x 1″
1 pair bread tongs	9¼″ x 1¼″
1 pair asparagus tongs	7⅞″ x 1¼″
1 pastry spatula	9⅞″ x 2″
1 steel	11½″ x 7/16″
1 nut cracker	6-5/16″ x 1″
1 bottle opener	5″ x 1⅜″
1 corkscrew	4¾″ x 2⅜″
1 pair grape scissors	8-1/16″ x 1-11/16″
1 pair sugar tongs	5½″ x 1-3/16″

LINEN

4 table cloths	folded to 15¾″ x 10½″
24 napkins	folded to 8¼″ square
4 tea table cloths	folded to 11″ x 7½″
24 tea napkins	folded to 5½″ square
2 table runners	folded to 14″ x 7½″

GLASSWARE

6 water goblets	d. 3⅜″ h. 6¾″
6 red wine glasses	d. 3″ h. 6-5/16″
6 white wine glasses	d. 2¾″ h. 5⅞″
6 champagne glasses	d. 3¾″ h. 5½″
6 liqueur glasses	d. 1-3/16″ h. 4″
6 cocktail glasses	d. 3-3/16″ h. 4¾″
6 tumblers	d. 2¾″ h. 3-9/16″
6 compote cups	d. 4¾″
1 compote bowl	d. 7½″
1 hors d'oeuvre-salad plate (in 4 pie-cut sections)	varied sizes, 15″ x 9″ maximum
1 salad bowl	d. 7½″—9″
1 pair oil and vinegar cruets	4¾″ x 2⅜″ h. 9″
1 salad dressing bowl	d. 4″
2 fruit bowls	d. 8″
1 cheese pot	d. 5″ h. 4″
1 breakfast set: butter dish	d. 7½″ h. 2¾″
marmalade dish	d. 4¾″ h. 4″
1 carafe	d. 4¾″—6″
1 wine decanter	d. 4¾″ h. 11″
1 glass cheese bell	d. 10¼″ h. 6¼″
1 salt cellar	d. 1⅝″ h. 13/16″
1 pepper cellar	d. 1⅝″ h. 13/16″

CHINAWARE

6 soup plates	d. 9½″ stacked: h. 2¾″
12 dinner plates	d. 9½″ stacked: h. 5″
12 salad-fruit plates	d. 8¼″ stacked: h. 4¾″
6 cake plates	d. 7⅛″—7½″ stacked: h. 4″
6 tea-coffee cups	d. 3½″—5″ h. 2″—3″ stack of 2: h. 3¼″—4″
6 tea-coffee saucers	d. 6″ stacked: h. 4″
1 tea pot	d. 10½″ h. 5½″
1 hot water pot	d. 4½″ h. 7″
1 creamer	d. 5⅛″ h. 3⅜″
1 sugar bowl	d. 3½″—6¼″ h. 3-3/16″—3-9/16″
6 demi-tasse cups	d. 2″—2¾″ h. 2⅛″ stack of 2: h. 3½″
6 demi-tasse saucers	d. 4¾″ stacked: h. 2″
1 coffee pot	d. 6½″ h. 7″
1 large milk pitcher	d. 5″ maximum
6 egg cups	d. 1¾″—2″ h. 2-9/16″—2¾″
2 oval platters	15⅜″ x 10¼″
1 fish platter	11¾″ x 7⅞″
1 round platter	d. 11¾″
1 pastry platter	d. 11″
1 soup tureen	d. 10⅝″—13″
1 vegetable dish	d. 7⅞″—10¼″
1 sauce boat	8¼″ x 5⅛″ h. 3½″
1 mustard pot	d. 2⅜″ h. 4″

SILVERWARE

6 napkin rings	d. 2⅜″
2 bottle trays	d. 6½″—7½″
trays: rectangular, round, oval	various sizes

INFORMAL SERVICE FOR 4

FLATWARE

4 breakfast spoons	7⅞″ x 1-3/16″
4 breakfast forks	8¼″ x 1-3/16″
4 dessert forks	5-5/16″ x 1-3/16″
4 breakfast knives	9-1/16″ x 1″
4 coffee spoons	5⅛″ x 1″
1 carving set: knife	11¾″ x 1-3/16″
fork	11½″ x ⅞″
1 salad set: spoon	8⅞″ x 1¾″
fork	8⅞″ x 1¾″
1 soup ladle	11-13/16″ x 2¾″
1 sauce ladle	7⅛″ x 2¾″

LINEN

2 table cloths	folded to 15¾″ x 10⅝″
8 napkins	folded to 8¼″ square

GLASSWARE

4 tumblers	d. 2¾″—3-3/16″ h. 3-9/16″—6-5/16″
1 carafe	d. 4¾″
1 pair oil and vinegar cruets	4¾″ x 2⅜″ h. 9″
1 salt cellar	d. 1⅝″ h. 13/16″
1 pepper cellar	d. 1⅝″ h. 13/16″

CHINAWARE

4 soup plates	d. 9½″ stacked: h. 1-15/16″
4 plates	d. 9½″ stacked: h. 1-15/16″
8 salad-dessert plates	d. 8¼″ stacked: h. 3½″
4 tea-coffee cups	d. 4″ h. 2″ stack of 2: h. 3¼″
4 tea-coffee saucers	d. 6″ stacked: h. 1⅝″
1 tea pot	d. 10½″—h. 5½″
1 coffee pot	d. 6½″—h. 7″
1 creamer	d. 5⅛″ h. 3⅜″
1 sugar bowl	d. 3½″ h. 3-3/16″
1 soup tureen	d. 10⅝″ h. 7⅛″
1 vegetable dish	d. 7⅞″ h. 4¾″
1 oval platter	11¾″ x 7⅞″
1 round platter	d. 11¾″

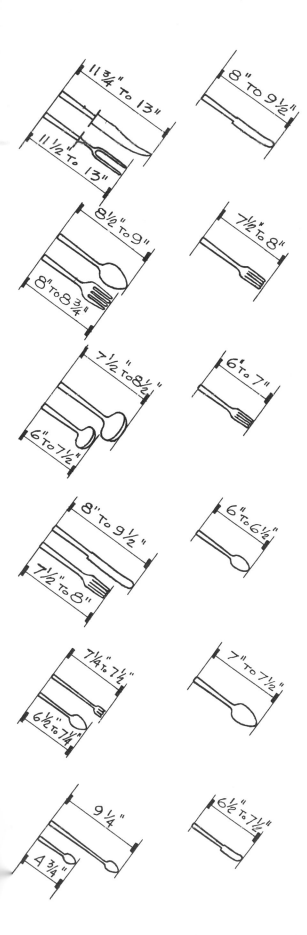

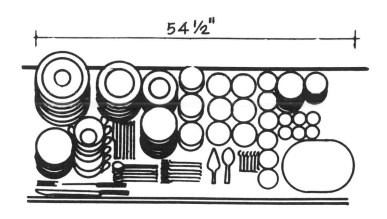

If all the dishes, cups, glasses, etc. used in a semi-formal dinner for six were spread out on one surface, they would occupy 24″ x 54½″ of storage.

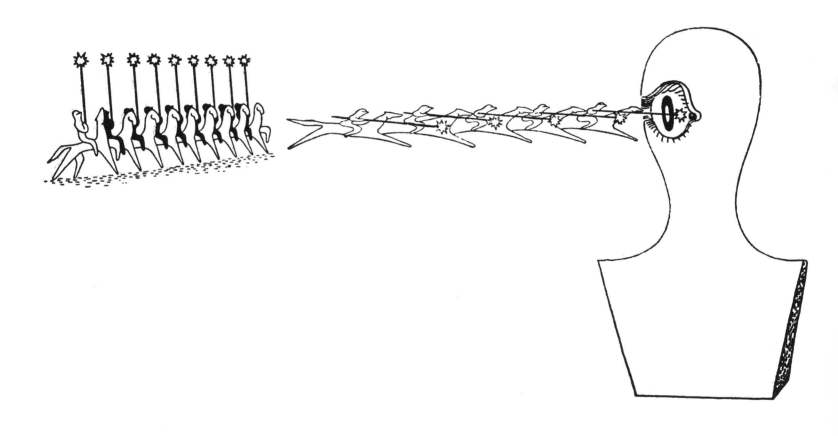

THE HUMAN EYE AND TELEVISION

The world-wide success of the motion picture and television industry is based on a fact that dice players, magicians, card sharps, and scenic designers have known for centuries: to wit, that the human eye is a very imperfect instrument. Not only is the hand quicker than the eye, but so are hundreds and hundreds of other objects.

The human eye suffers from, or rejoices in, what scientists call "persistence of vision." It cannot digest more than sixteen separate pictures passing before it in one second. If a regularly spaced succession of pictures is flashed before the eye at that speed or greater, the brain gets an impression of continuous motion. Logically, therefore, sixteen frames to the second is the speed of the standard movie camera. The iconoscope or camera tube works on the same principle. It transmits a series of separate pictures, but does it faster.

For your information, the basic principle of television was understood almost as far back as that of the telephone. In 1886 a character named Nipkow invented a scanning disk which was a flat pie plate with a concentric series of small square holes. It revolved at a speed of 20 turns per second, covering the entire surface of a picture through its apertures in one second. The picture thus covered could, in theory, be transmitted over a wire to a receiving disc traveling at the same speed in front of a photographic plate. The only trouble with the Nipkow system was that it depended on extraordinary accuracy in the size of the holes in the two disks, and equal accuracy in the speed of the motors that controlled their revolutions.

Tentative suggestions: 1. Let the sun or other light in. 2. Anchor your set, not your chairs, which should be light and easy to move. 3. Illustrator Repetto offers the two-way settee so that some may contemplate the fire while other contemplate the Mets. 4. Engineers suggest that the eye may be rested by the presence of some other focus of attention: picture, statue, or whatever.

Do not be disturbed if the image in the human eye is upside down compared to the vision in the television tube. The eye's lens is like a camera lens. It sees everything upside down but there is a sort of back switch in the optic nerves that flops the thing right side up again.

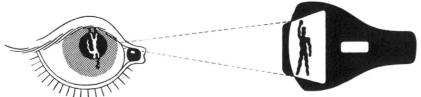

The illustration shows some of the quandaries that arise in the installation of a television set in a private home, but the saloon keeper has all of these problems and many more.

So that our saloon keeper's clientele can keep the use of its collective eyes for as long as possible, he must buy the set with the largest viewing tube that he can afford. The set then has to be placed high on the wall for viewing over fedoras and alcoholic fumes. This however, increases visual distortion.

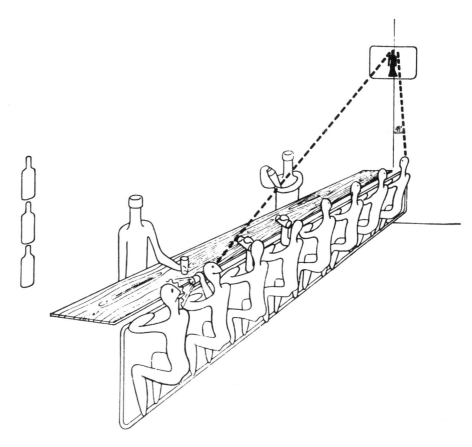

Of the bottle-shaped habitués, the two closest to the tube are too near and too far below it. This space is virtually wasted. Those at the farthest left are too far away. The four in the center are correctly placed, but now we have a psychological problem: two are so crazy about the program they spill their drinks and forget the reorder. The other two hate it, and so why did the saloon keeper buy the set in the first place?

Ophthalmologists and television technicians are agreed that the best way to avoid television eye fatigue is to stay away from the set. Since all eyes are different, the correct distance is difficult to determine. The room illustrated below shows good seating arrangements for today's large-tube sets. Try to avoid seating anyone at an angle of more than 30° from the center of vision. Of course, as our drawing shows, farsighted people should sit even further back but nearsighted people should not get too close.

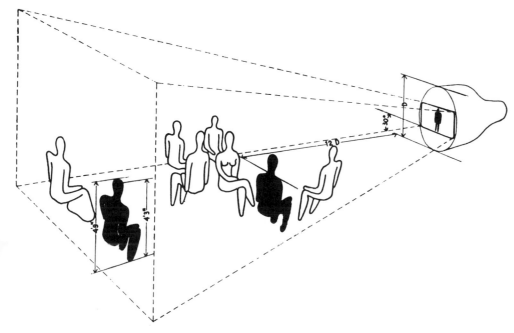

COMMERCIAL APPLICATIONS

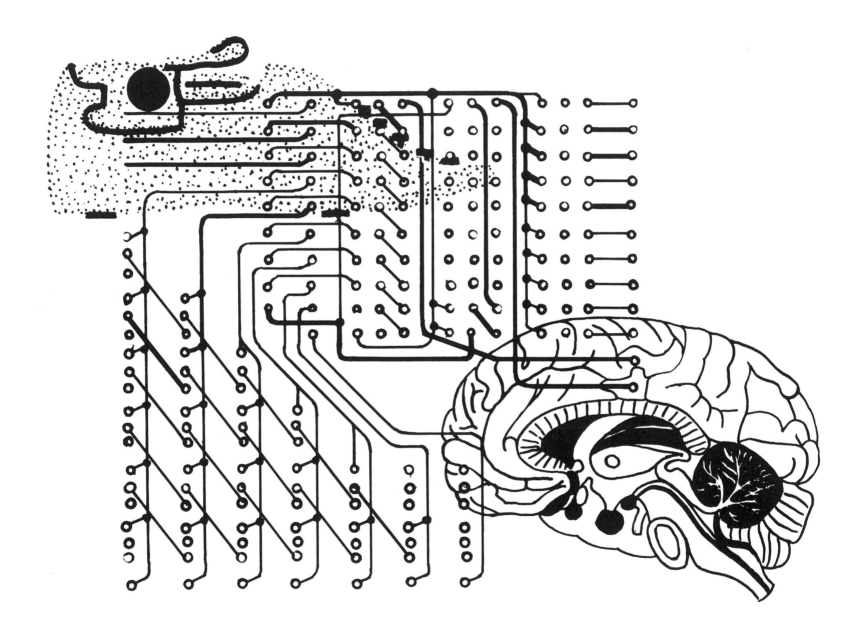

THE BUSINESS OFFICE

The popularity of the office party is so great that it is often no longer confined to Christmas. Clerks, stenographers, salesmen, executives, and even accountants are finding more and more opportunities for getting loaded together. It is perhaps for this reason more than any other that, as office space becomes dearer, each individual worker, while forced by circumstances to be nearer his neighbor, needs the modern equivalent of a bundling board to separate himself as much as possible from the neighbor. This is clearly a development of the party system because (a) The chasee of the previous night does not want to have to listen to the excuses of the chaser (particularly if the chaser was caught); (b) The chaser wants to be able to get away and hide until he or she thinks up a good excuse.

We are not absolutely certain that manufacturers of furniture and equipment have recognized all the nuances arising from these activities but our measurements will help designers arrange units in logical ways—to provide the proper party atmosphere when occasion demands. No-one need worry about whether the furniture or equipment functions for work **and** play; our office worker community is quite original in the art of adaptation.

It is the constant boast of manufacturers of office furniture that no other branch of the furniture industry has made more careful anatomical studies, or done more research on the functional use of drawers, shelves and lighting, the dimensions of telephones, ledgers, stationery, etc. than they have.

For designers who would build their own, or manufacturers who might change their lines, we present these dimensional drawings.

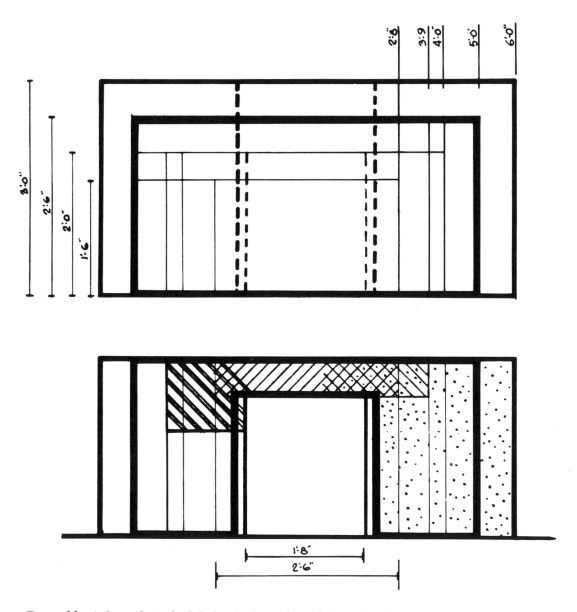

Top and front views of standard desks, the heavy lines designating the proportions most generally used.

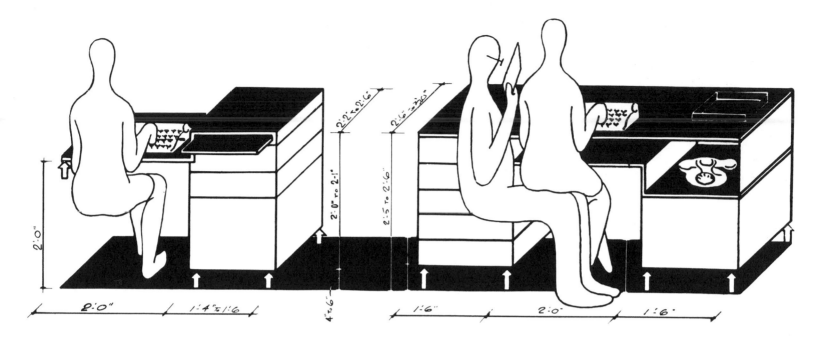

Note that the typewriter shelf of a stenographer's desk should be 3¼ inches below the normal desk top. Otherwise the only way the young lady can type is in the position shown above, a position frowned upon in many conservative offices.

The plight of the little clerk, overworked at his little table, and the big boss, with one letter to sign on his big desk, are here most graphically illustrated.

Office furniture is functional, and it should be efficient, but it may have sharp corners. The 3'-4" for passageway directly below is a most important measurement. Drawing at left illustrates the proper height of counters and shelves.

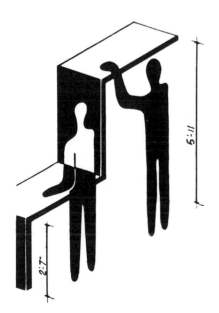

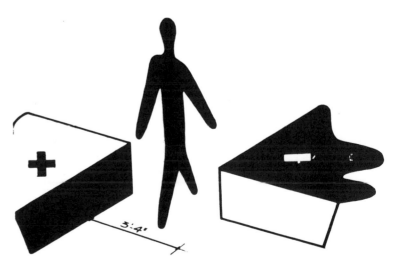

Possibly one of the most useful drawings in the entire book is this on shelving. Remembering the reach of the typical office girl or library assistant, the top shelf of a stack should not be more than 5'-8" above the floor. Allow at least 3 feet for rump room between the stacks, double it where open shelves are on both sides. The drawing at right gives standard sizes of books from duodecimo to elephant folio.

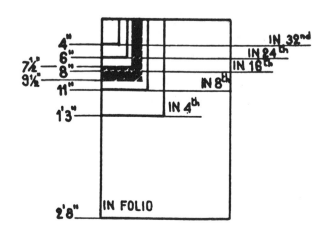

The file cabinet is undoubtedly the most frequently used or misused piece of office equipment available. The following pages show some of the standard measurements involved as well as Nino's idea of an efficiency expert's nightmare.

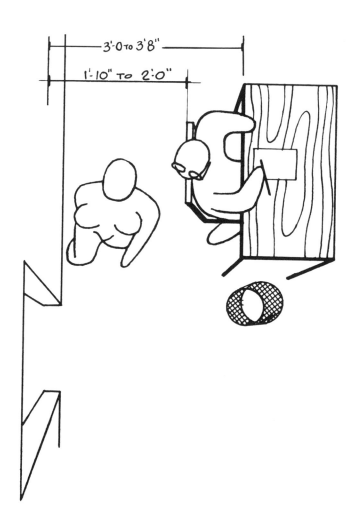

Diagram illustrates the distance required by a headless stuffed shirt from behind his desk to the nearest wall or obstruction assuming no passage required.

To permit comfortable ogling a bald-headed clerk requires a total distance from behind his desk to the nearest obstruction of from 3'-0" to 3'-8" if passage is required.

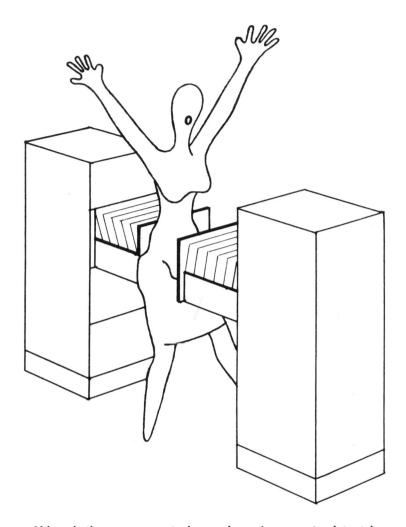

Although the arrangement shown above is guaranteed to take inches off the waist, it tends to impede office traffic. Adequate clearance should be provided to allow passage between two banks of files.

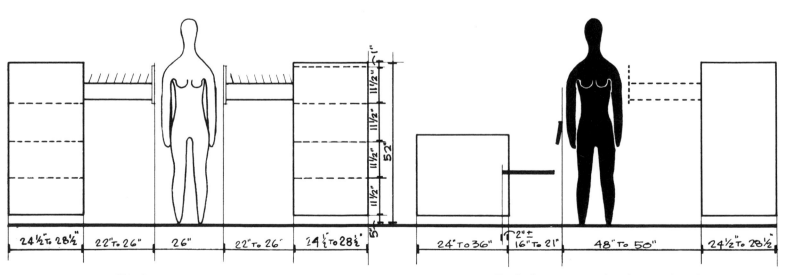

Open file plus passage plus open file.   **Desk plus passage plus drawer plus file.**

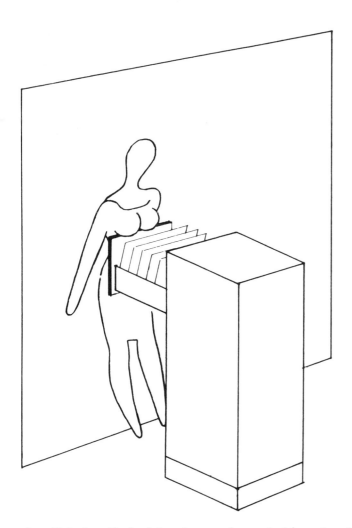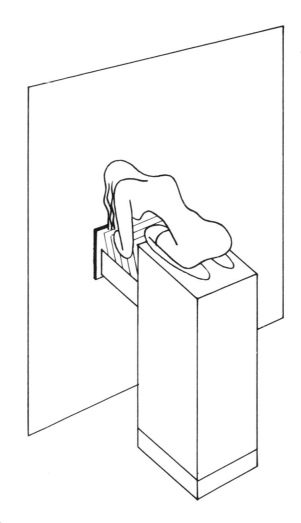

An efficient method of insuring good secretarial posture is to allow inadequate clearance for access behind file drawer, as shown above. The position assumed at right would be quite appropriate for the annual Christmas party but a bit too much for day to day office routine. Clearance should be at least 4 feet.

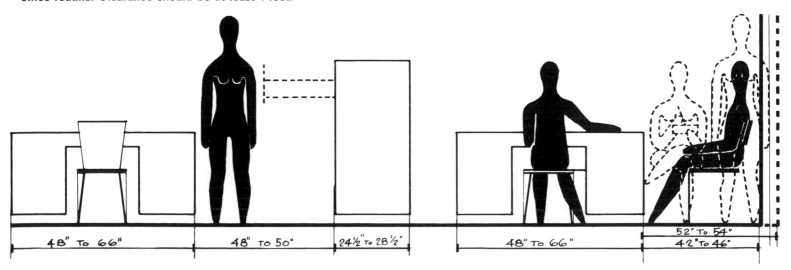

48" TO 66"   48" TO 50"   24½" TO 28½"

Desk plus chair plus passage plus file.

48" TO 66"   52" TO 54"
               42" TO 46"

Desk plus chair plus passage.

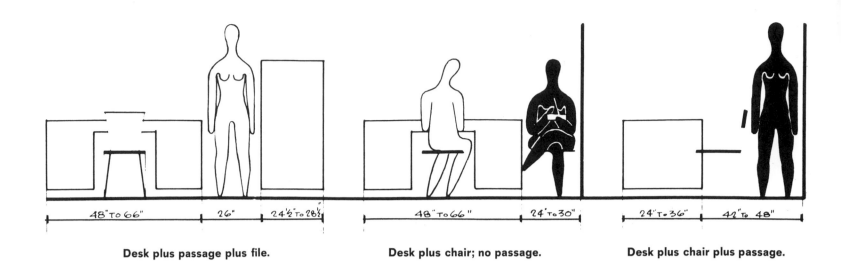

Desk plus passage plus file. 48"to 66" 26" 24½"to 28½"

Desk plus chair; no passage. 48"to 66" 24"to 30"

Desk plus chair plus passage. 24"to 36" 42"to 48"

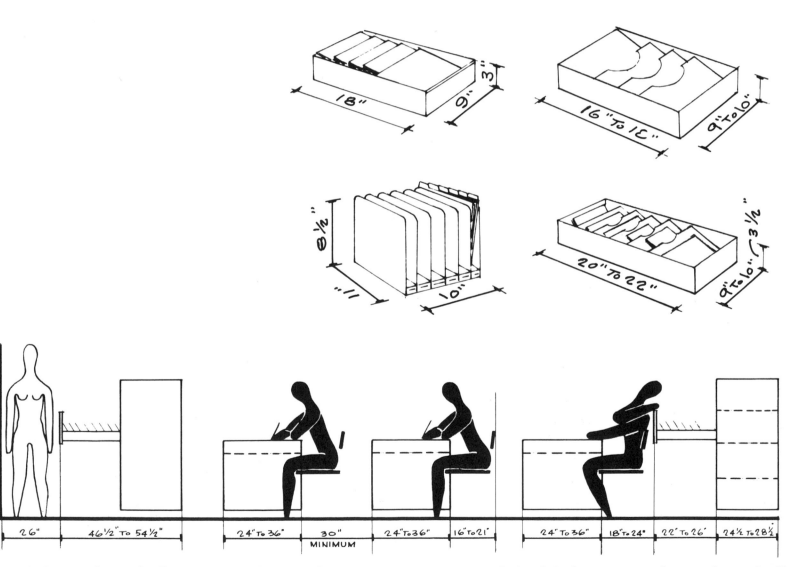

18" 9" 3"

16"to 18" 9"to 10"

8½" 11" 10"

20"to 22" 9"to 10" 3½"

Desk plus open drawer plus file. 26" 46½"to 54½"

Desks in a row. 24"to 36" 30" MINIMUM 24"to 36" 16"to 21"

Desk plus chair plus no passage plus open drawer plus file. 24"to 36" 18"to 24" 22"to 26" 24½"to 28½"

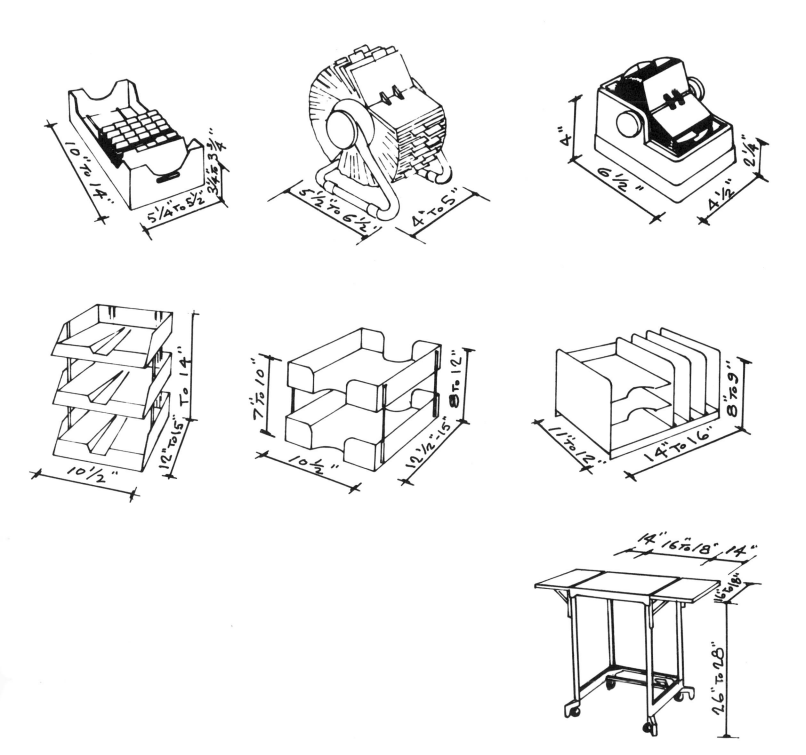

10" to 14"   5¼" To 5½"   3¼" to 3¾"

5½" To 6½"   4" To 5"

4"   6½"   4½"   2¼"

12" To 15"   To 14"   10½"

7" To 10"   10½"   12½"-15"   8 To 12"

11" To 12"   14" To 16"   8 To 9"

14"   16 To 18"   14"   16 To 18"   26" To 28"

THE RETAIL STORE

For the benefit of more reactionary readers the diagram across indicates the basic design criteria relative to contemporary pushcart planning. The model depicted comes equipped with Jaguar fenders and custom-made tail fins of any description.

However, for lovers of the soft sell and more conventional retail store facilities we have suggested on the following pages varied criteria, ranging from the typical dimensions of a wrapping counter to the layout of a 3-way dressing room mirror.

The diagrams on the following pages illustrate some of the more usual layout conditions found in the retail store. It is important to note that the dimensions indicated are not to be rigidly interpreted but should serve rather as a basic point of departure in the preliminary planning of the space involved.

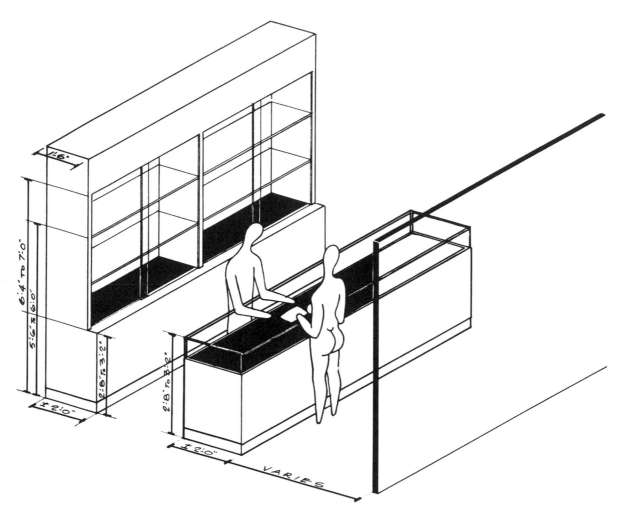

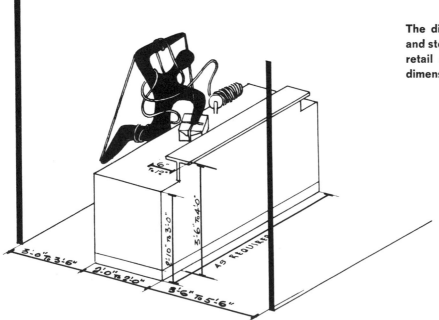

The diagram above indicates a fairly common counter showcase and storage combination that could apply to a number of diversified retail store operations. The figure at left illustrates the critical dimensions for a typical wrapping counter.

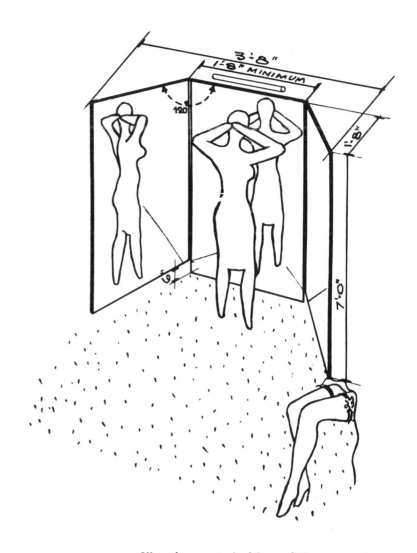
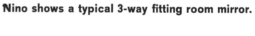

Nino shows a typical 3-way fitting room mirror.

Shopping for shoes can be far less trying for both the customer and the salesman if the minimum clearances indicated on the drawing below are maintained.

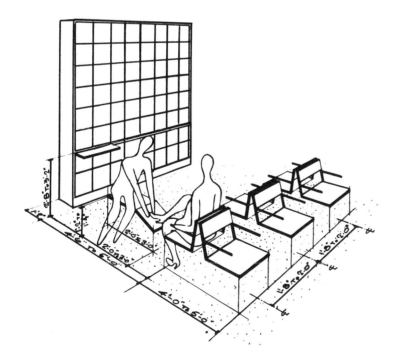

RESTAURANTS AND BARS

His day half done, the average man goes out to lunch, but before we go into the immediate problems of restaurant design, and that is a big subject indeed, a word about the drawing. Mr. Repetto calls it the battle between the Christians and the turkeys and, as anyone who has studied early Christian art knows, some of the knights in those days rode steeds of about as much substance as the mounts Nino has supplied his Christians. As for the turkeys, well, the chef is in hot pursuit. Remember all this when you order your next turkey sandwich. For the proportions of bars, soda fountains, lunch counters we are greatly indebted to the Brunswick-Balke-Collender Co. In the simple matter of restaurant tables and chairs, two important facts have not been illustrated. The standard sizes for two and four place restaurant tables are: 20" x 20"; 20" x 40"; and a 40" diameter circle. If restaurant chairs with arms are chosen be sure that the arms fit under the table top, to have floor space when it is not in use.

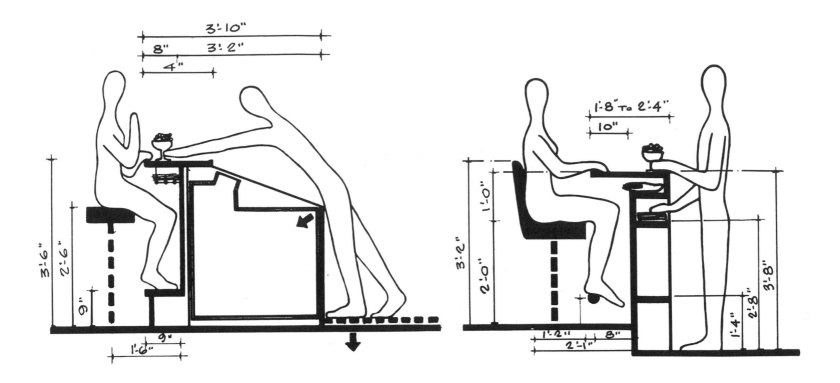

Above, the soda fountain. Note large space needed for ice cream cooler. Below, the low 2-foot stool, suitable for the traditional 3-foot lunch counter, is objected to by some nervous Nellies lest soda jerks squint down the fronts of their dresses. Our suggestion would be to make the clerks either shorter or older.

The lunch counter, more elaborate than the one shown at left, below, and the beer bar, below. Space between footrail and face of bar (to prevent scuffing) is very important, as is the glove compartment under the lunch counter's top.

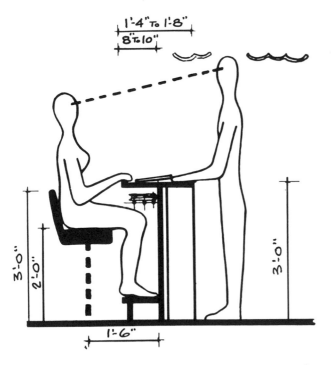

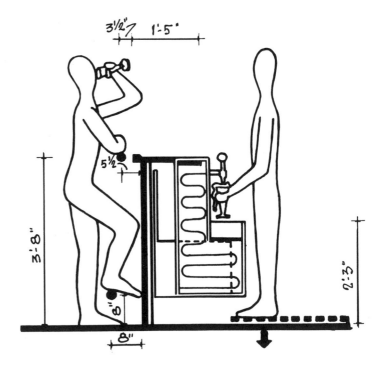

If the customer, who is demonstrably half full already, studied this diagram carefully he could learn everything he ought to know about the appurtenances of perpendicular drinking, from back bar and duckboards to beer cooler and bar stool. Note particularly the 4-inch mixing shelf, and the proper height for bottle and glass shelving.

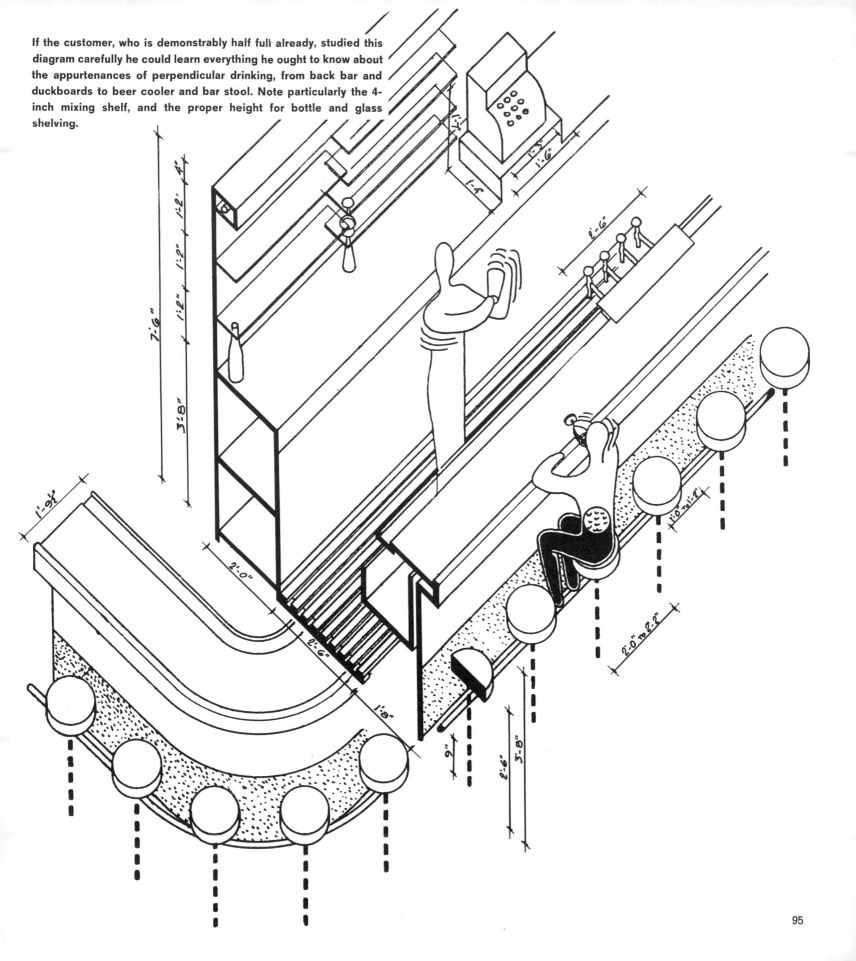

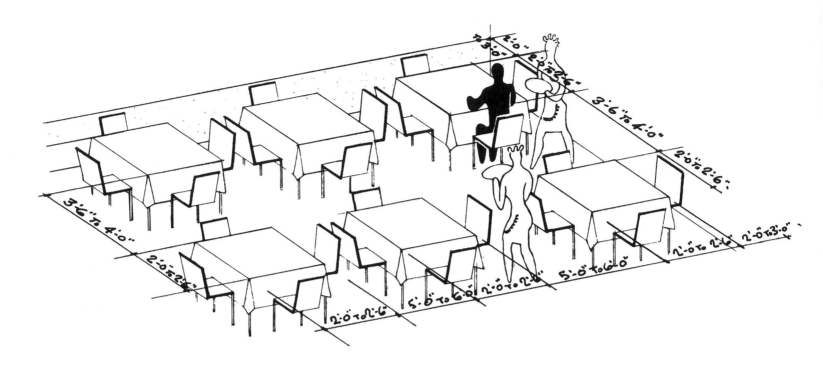

In the drawing above Repetto shows that table arrangements must allow minimum aisle widths for service and public while the figures on this simple drawing tell how much space an insulted lady needs to leave the room; the size of a restaurant table top, the diameter of a wolf's smile, and the area occupied by a waiter with a check.

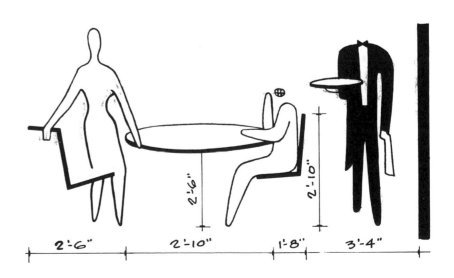

An angled or diagonal table layout (below) is rather common. Minimum clearances are indicated.

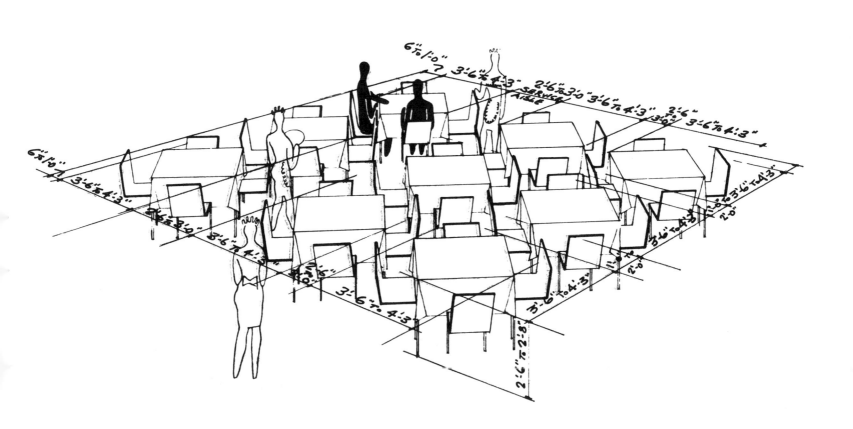

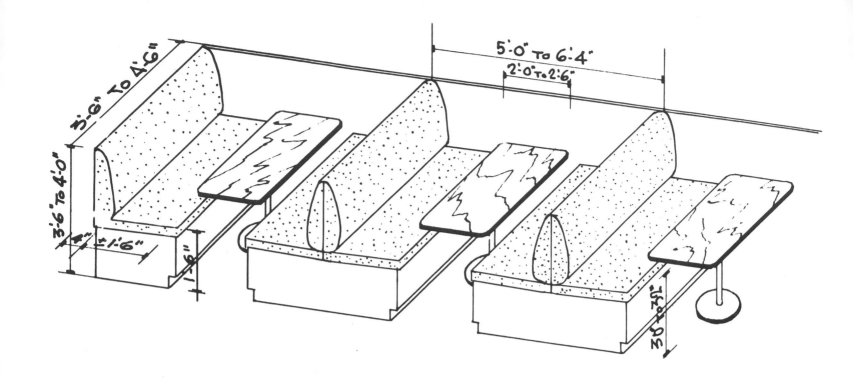

The comfort and privacy of continuous wall seating may be debatable, and rightly so, but it really packs them in. If job conditions dictate this type of arrangement the measurements shown can be used as a minimum point of departure for design purposes. The drawing below indicates the critical measurements of a banquette arrangement.

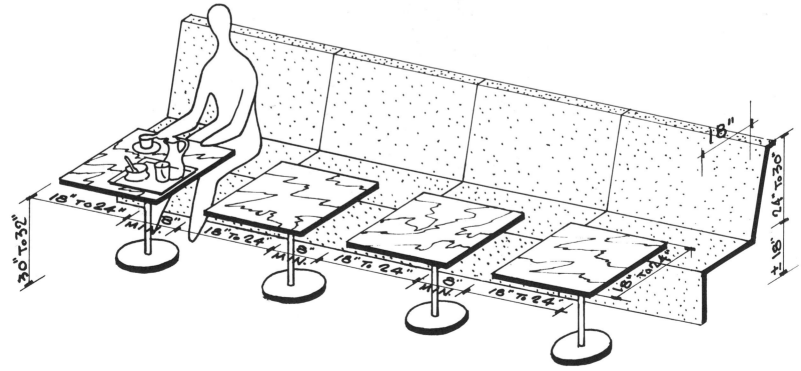

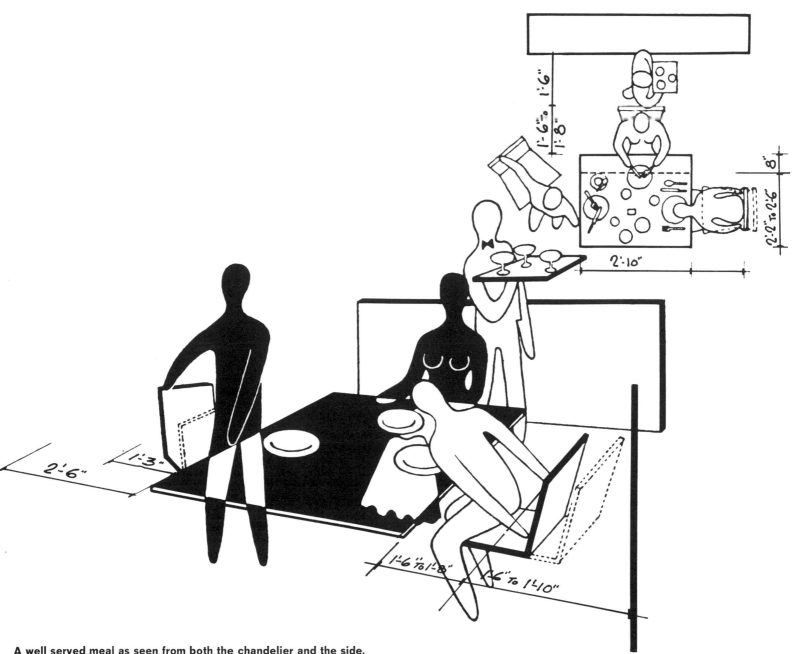

A well served meal as seen from both the chandelier and the side, requires adequate space not only for dishes, diners, and servers but also for their movements.

CIRCULATION

HORIZONTAL AND VERTICAL

Horizontal movement is something that everyone thinks he knows about; vertical movement conjures up visions of levitation. We are writing about neither interpretation but about rather more pedestrian meanings of the subjects. It takes only about 2 minutes to travel nearly ¼ mile from the ground floor to the 102nd floor of the Empire State Building — and this includes two changes of elevators. If Frank Lloyd Wright had built his mile-high skyscraper it would have been possible to get from the ground to the top in something like 7 minutes. To travel distances like these on the surface in a busy city, as everybody knows who has tried it, takes an awful lot longer. Nor is getting there half the fun.

A substantial portion of interior design projects involve major modifications to existing multi-story structures. In these instances, not only must the designer consider flow within functional areas on each floor, but he must also consider the problem of vertical circulation between the various levels themselves, in terms of stairs, moving stairs, and elevators.

The designer is not usually required, except perhaps in large offices where there is a well-staffed architectural department, to prepare detailed working drawings of such installations. Technical consultation and assistance is always available from practicing architects or the engineering departments of the manufacturer involved.

It is essential, however, that the designer be conversant with the terminology and the more elementary design criteria involved. Moreover, he should be knowledgeable enough to make preliminary judgments about such items as type of system and feasibility of the installation. The designer should also have some idea of the approximate costs of such installations, at least to the extent of establishing budget figures.

On the opposite page, for future consideration, we have provided details of what we think will be all the rage in Post World War III vertical circulation systems.

On the following pages, and for your more immediate use, we have provided certain illustrations on the planning of more contemporary systems, including three methods to physically incapacitate your client through poor stair design. Have fun . . .

From observation, it can be readily seen that the run of the stair is equal to the total sum of the width of all the individual treads. Similarly the rise of the stair is equal to the total sum of all the heights of the individual risers or the distance between floors. The **headroom** is the vertical distance between the clearing of the upper level and a point directly under.

Stairs may be generally classified as open or closed. Both open and closed may be any of the general types shown in these illustrations.

The size of the stair treads and risers vary and are determined largely by the rise and run of the stair. Normally, treads are between 9½ inches and 12 inches wide and risers between 7 inches and 8 inches high. In monumental design, risers may be as shallow as 6 inches and treads as wide as 16 inches.

Step 1. Determine heights of riser desired in inches (7 inches to 8 inches).

Step 2. Convert rise to inches.

Step 3. Divide rise in inches by riser in inches to obtain number of rises.

Step 4. Since there is always one more riser than treads, subtract 1 from the number of risers to obtain the number of treads.

The important thing in designing a staircase is to decide how many people are going to use it. If only two people are likely to pass at one time, 4'-3" is wide enough. If three people are to use a stair, add another 2 feet. Note that for schools, and places where many children gather, hand rails should be 8" lower than the standard 2'-10". In all cases the minimum depth of landings should be at least equal to the width of the stair.

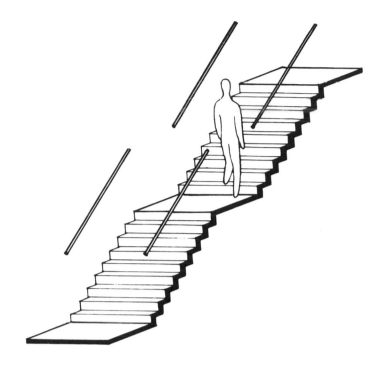

The stair above is a variation of the one shown at the left. The difference is the introduction of an intermediate landing. This platform is ordinarily introduced when floor-to-floor height exceeds 12 feet. The variation shown below differs in that the second run takes off to the right instead of doubling back on itself. This design may be employed either to meet a specific planning condition or for completely esthetic considerations.

On these and the next two pages we show the various types of stair design ranging from that above which, though it occupies more space lengthwise, provides a simple and straightforward means of vertical circulation and is the most economical in construction. Of course this one is better for kangaroos than for people because it exceeds the 12 foot rise beyond which a stair should be provided with a landing.

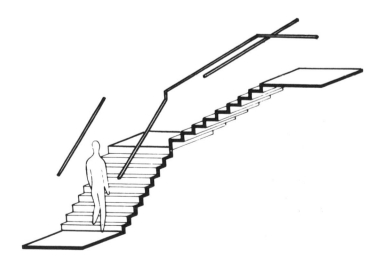

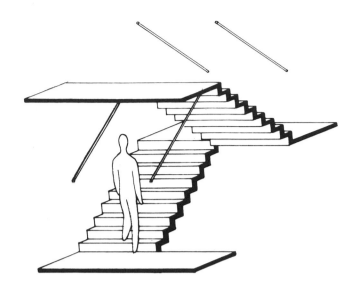

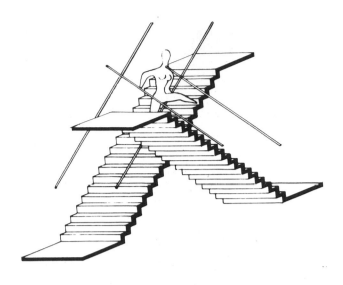

The design shown above, left, has two advantages. By providing an intermediary landing between floors it permits less tiresome ascent. Since the stair doubles back on itself it occupies less room in one direction. It does, however, require greater width. In any event, depending on existing space available, it can be both a space saver and a painless method of getting up in the world. At right is the "scissor" stair which is an excellent way of providing two completely private means of vertical circulation within the same construction complex. They are often used to satisfy requirements for two exits when called for in the local building code.

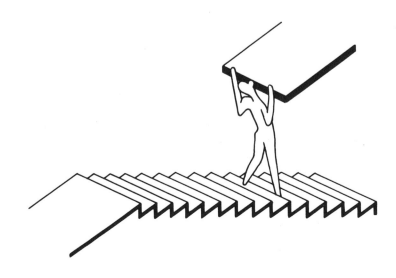

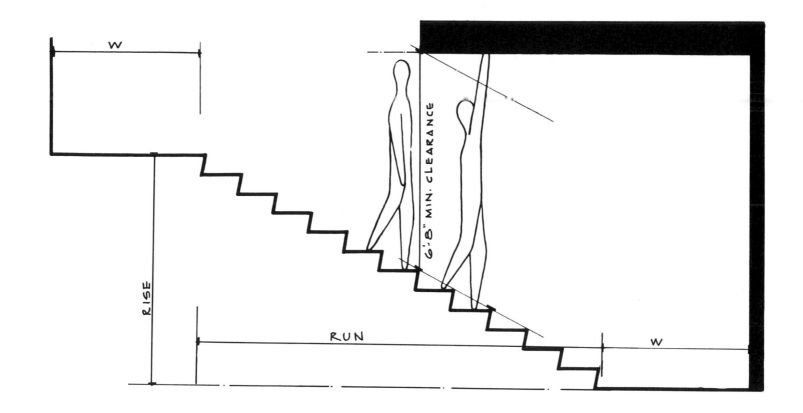

Since the 6'-8" basketball player is used to socking his head on pendant light fixtures and other "low bridges" of various kinds, he might forgive a designer who allowed the minimum clearances shown above. 6-foot characters would only be bruised psychologically; nevertheless, they would be happier if clearances were over 7 feet.

THREE WAYS TO PHYSICALLY INCAPACITATE A CLIENT

Left, design stair landing as shown so that dimension "W" is less than width of stair. This condition will insure multiple lacerations and contusions about the face and body.

Center, if it is desired to localize client injury to the region of the head, allow inadequate headroom. This probably constitutes the most direct approach and any clearance of less than 6'-8" should easily do the job.

Right, a comparatively sneaky tactic is to incorporate a sudden change in stride in your design. This method never fails if you have a flair for the dramatic for when properly executed the client will rebound from several walls before completing his descent.

Elevators, as a means of vertical circulation, should incorporate immediate access to cars at any floor, constant speed, and deceleration periods, smooth, quiet, comfortable, and speedy transportation, and closeting, on a lucky day, with an attractive companion. The technical considerations involved in elevator installation are beyond our scope here but the proper selection and the specifications for installation must be predicated on a detailed analysis of the traffic and an evaluation of the standard type of machinery and controls that would be applicable. As in the preceding chapters, we shall here concern ourselves only with anatomical matters.

Elevators, unlike moving stairs, which are discussed below, require hoistways necessitating the construction of continuous vertical shafts from the lower floors to the upper floors. In existing structures this would make installations almost impossible without relocating existing facilities in its path.

The dimensions of hoistways may vary from a width of 4'-2" and depth of 3'-10½" for a small residential installation to corresponding dimensions of 8'-4" and 7'-6" for a large office building installation. Standard dimensions for elevators have been agreed upon by the National Elevator Manufacturers Industry (N.E.M.I.).

The moving stairway is now and probably will be until we develop wings or personal engines a fairly common means of vertical transportation. It is

The pure spiral is often used for purely esthetic reasons but it is also very useful when space is at a premium.

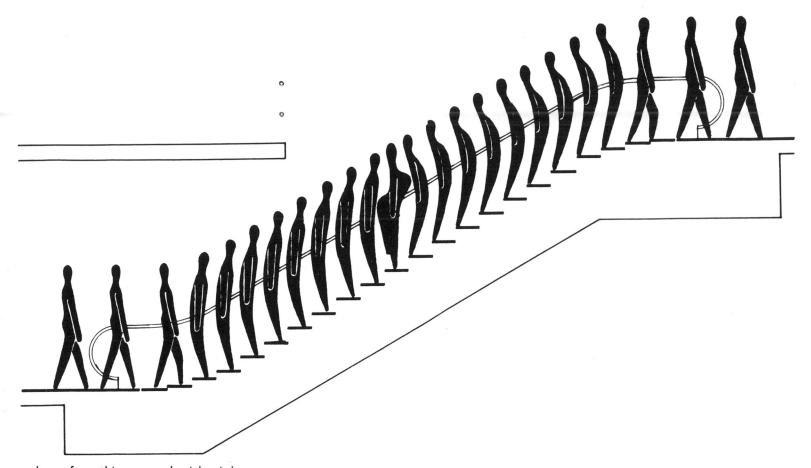

also referred to as an electric stairway. Such installations are most useful where there is a relatively uniform traffic load continuously on the move in both directions.

The most common use of the moving stairway is in large department stores, in office buildings, to connect lobby floors with mezzanines, to connect the various levels of rail or bus or air terminals, and, more recently, in school buildings. Installations are most common in buildings of relatively few floors. While liable to cause traumas in old ladies and visions of slow mangling to wearers of spike-heeled shoes, moving stairways are the delight of all children under twelve without attendant mothers. Another attendant advantage is the constant rate of speed with which passengers are received and discharged and the consequent elimination of backlogging and congestion at landings. Still another advantage, at least in comparison with the elevator, is the fact that its location can be staggered throughout the floors—an important factor in conversion jobs.

Moving stair installations are usually of two types—the scissors type and the parallel type, both of which are shown here. The scissors type criss-crosses the up and down banks. In both types of installations the stairs can be located adjacent to each other or far apart as may be desired.

The stairs usually come in three standard widths of 2'-6", 3'-0" and 4'-0" and are installed at an angle of 30°. Under normal traffic conditions, the lower banks of stairs are usually larger in width than the upper banks.

Structurally, the moving stairway is normally supported by trusses built into the unit, which in turn are tied in with the structural system of the building.

Moving stairs of 2½ foot, 3 foot and 4 foot widths can carry four, six and eight thousand people per hour. The floor opening required is about 14'-6" x 4'-4". The drawing right shows the critical dimensions and clearances involved.

In costing, an approximation for a 30-inch stair would be $25-$30,000 for the first ten feet of run and between $750 and $1,000 for each additional foot. For a 48-inch stair, the corresponding figures would be between $30-$35,000 for the first 10 feet and between $1,000 and $1,250 for each additional foot. Since costs vary constantly it is advised that current prices be checked with the local distributor involved.

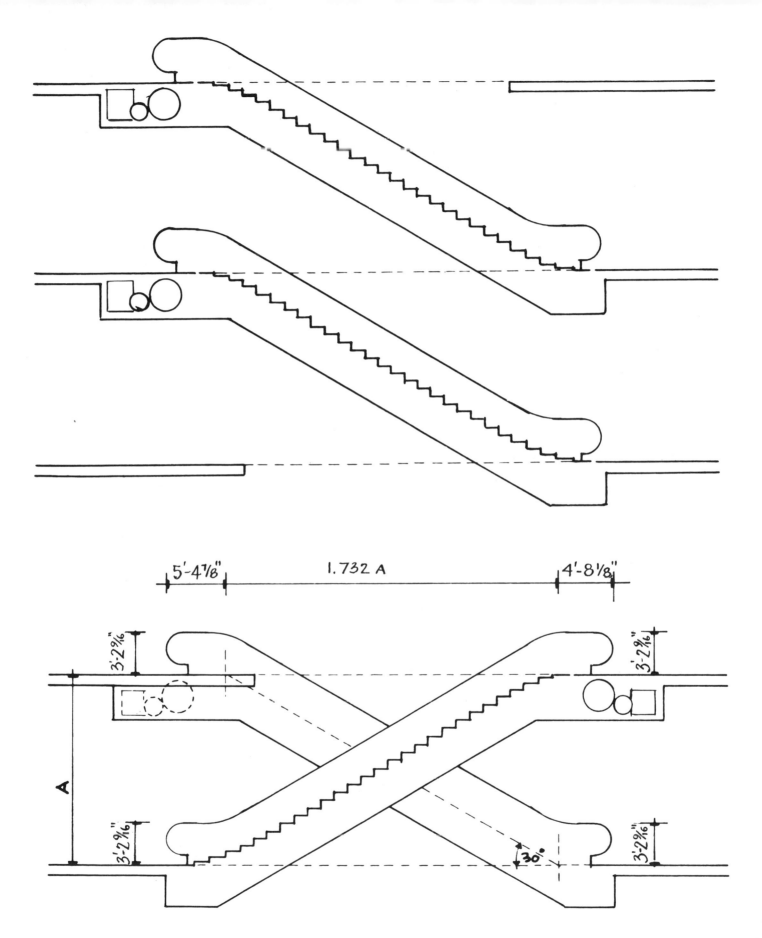

5'-4⅞"   1.732 A   4'-8⅛"

3'-2⁹⁄₁₆"   3'-2⁹⁄₁₆"

A

3'-2⁹⁄₁₆"   30°   3'-2⁹⁄₁₆"

One of the most important considerations when providing elevators as the primary means of vertical circulation is adequate lobby space. Approximately 4 to 5 square feet per person should be allowed for passengers waiting at any bank of elevators. Similarly the corridors should also allow 4 to 5 square feet for passengers approaching the lobby. The determination of the number of passengers should be based on a traffic check at a 15 to 20 minute peak period of a peak hour.

That a space allowance of from 4 to 5 square feet per passenger should be provided in elevator lobby design is the message that the anti-social characters depicted at left are trying to get across. The number of passengers should be based on a 15 to 20 minute peak period. A sure way to provide for planned confusion, congestion, and chaos is to allow inadequate elevator lobby and corridor space.

A mass of useful information will be found in this diagram from the correct height for doorbells to the amount of space needed to kiss a lady's hand. It is interesting, and may be useful, to know that it takes only 6 inches more floor space to have someone help you into your coat than to struggle into it yourself.

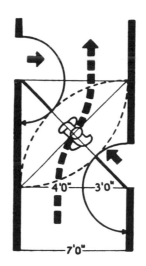

The diagram at right is not a Saturday night exercise in how to avoid swinging doors, but a note to designers of hotel and office building corridors to stagger opposite doors whenever possible, so that, as in this case, a 7 foot corridor can do the work of an 8 foot corridor.

Almost any kind of passageway and corridor can be laid out from this diagram from a narrow aisle between shop counters to the 7'-11" necessary when two opposite doors open outward.

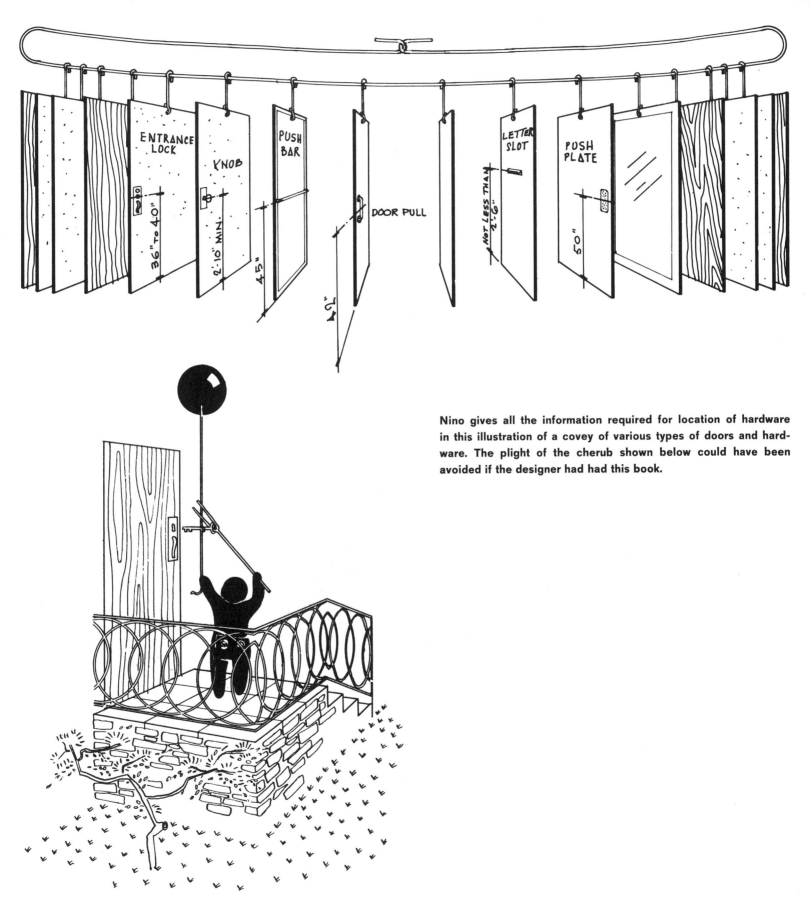

Nino gives all the information required for location of hardware in this illustration of a covey of various types of doors and hardware. The plight of the cherub shown below could have been avoided if the designer had had this book.

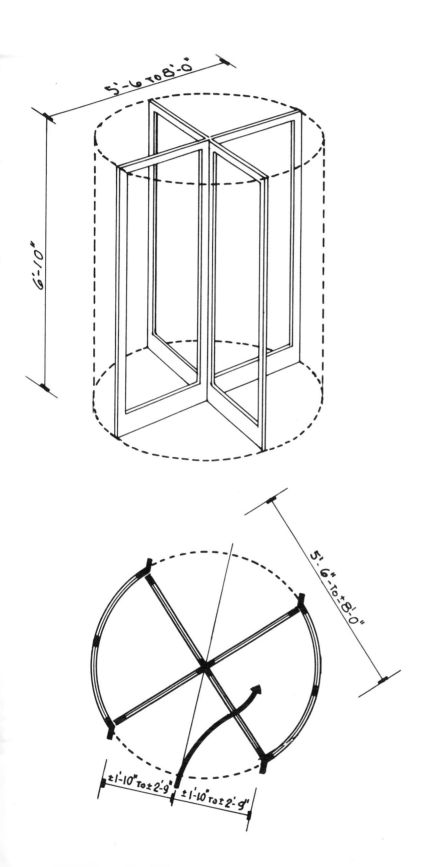

5'-6" to 8'-0"

6'-10"

5'-6" To ± 8'-0"

± 1'-10" To ± 2'-9"   ± 1'-10" To ± 2'-9"

Drawing at left gives critical dimensions for revolving doors.

LIGHTING

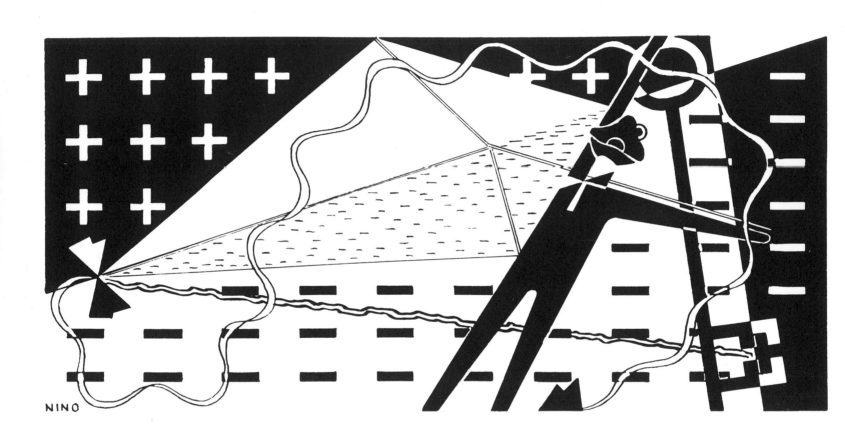

NINO

IMPORTANCE AND EFFECT

The American-based author of this book has lately found that during his working hours in public and commercial buildings he is being deprived of any place to hide and, what's more, his shadow appears only during the rare intervals when he escapes from under luminous ceilings. On the other hand, when he goes hunting in the modern manner for food or liquid viands, he more often than not has to produce a flashlight to find his way to a table. His question is two-fold: (a) is his shadow being used for possibly satanic purposes during the hours when it does not appear to be in his possession, and (b) are restaurants and bars **really** getting darker or is his night vision being impaired by daylight lighting? Will carrot juice help? After this plea to Bernarr MacFadden, let us turn to some rather more pleasant consideration of lighting.

Perhaps one of the most important elements in the design of interiors is form —be it the form of the room itself or that of the objects contained within it. The relationship of these forms, in terms of function and esthetics, can well decide the relative success or failure of any interior design project. It is apparent that of the five senses the sense of sight plays a dominant role in the interpretation of form. It should be noted, however, that since the eye is dependent on light, the nature of the lighting design within a room can cause varied interpretations of the same form.

The table, chair, or ceramic pottery that one may place in a room can only be seen and its form interpreted by the observer because it reflects the light rays hitting its surface. The source of these rays may be the sun or an artificial light source in the room and the rays emitted may hit the object directly or may be reflected from other surfaces around it.

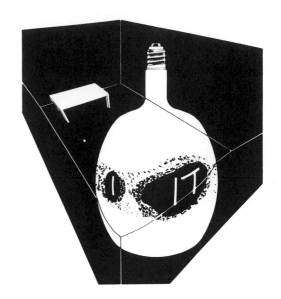

The color and texture of the object itself and its surrounding surfaces can affect the degree to which the light rays are reflected and, indirectly, the interpretation of the form being observed.

If we were to place a small coffee table within a room the walls, floors and ceiling of which were painted an intense black color and then illuminate the room with a single lamp light source to the right of center, the form of the table would appear to the observer somewhat as shown above. The effect is due to the fact that the only surfaces actually illuminated are those that face the light source. Those that do not are left in total darkness.

On the other hand, if the room were painted white, the rays from the light source, in addition to reflecting directly off the object, would also be reflected from the wall, floor, and ceiling surfaces behind and around the object thus illuminating all of its surfaces.

It is beyond the scope of this book to explore very deeply the relationship between the interpretation of form and lighting design; we can only stress its importance and illustrate some of the more dramatic effects possible.

This poor soul in the illustration below is basking in a pretty good example of direct lighting while the two characters above depict one possible result of indirect lighting.

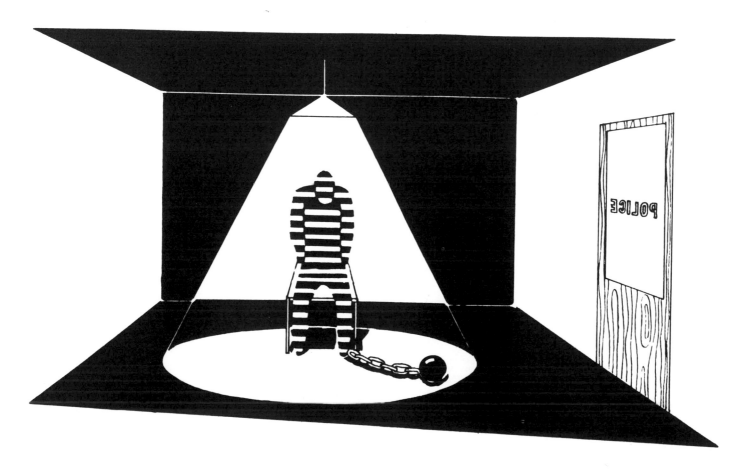

MEASUREMENT

The level of illumination is measured in foot-candles—a foot-candle being the direct illumination on a surface everywhere one foot from a uniform point source of one international candle. The following table indicates the foot-candle power per square foot recommended for different functional areas. Levels given below are taken from the report of the Illuminating Engineering Society's Committee on Recommendations for Quantity and Quality of Illumination which were published in the Society's journal, Illuminating Engineering, Volume LIII, Number 8 and Volume LIV, Number 2.

	Footcandles
ART GALLERIES	
General	30
On paintings (supplementary)	30-100
On statuary and other displays	100-200
AUDITORIUMS	
Assembly	15
Exhibition	30
BANKS	
General	50-70
Tellers' stations	150
Regular office work	100
CHURCHES AND SYNAGOGUES	
Altar, ark, reredos	100
Classrooms	30
Pulpit, rostrum (supplementary illumination)	50
Main worship area	15-30
Art glass windows (test recommended)	
Light color	50
Medium color	100
Dark color	500
Especially dense windows	1000
DENTAL CLINICS	
Waiting room	
General	15
Reading	30
Operatory, general	70
Instrument cabinet	150
Dental chair	1000
Laboratory, bench	100
Recovery room	5
DEPOTS, TERMINALS, AND STATIONS	
Waiting room	30
Ticket offices	
General	100
Ticket rack and counters	100
HOMES	
Entrances, hallways, stairways, stair landings, living room, dining room, bedroom, family room, sun room, library, game or recreation room	
General illumination	10
Reading and writing, including studying	
Books, magazines, newspapers	30
Handwriting, reproduction and poor copies	70
Desks, study	70

	Footcandles
Reading music scores	
Simple scores	30
Advanced scores	70
Kitchen activities	
Sink	70
Range and work surfaces	50
Laundry, trays, ironing board, ironer	50
Sewing	
Dark fabrics (fine detail, low contrast)	200
Prolonged periods (light to medium fabrics)	100
Occasional periods	30-50
Shaving, make-up, grooming; on the face at mirror locations	50
Work shop, bench work	70
HOSPITALS	
Anesthetizing and preparation room	30
Autopsy	
Autopsy room	100
Autopsy table	2500
Corridor	
General	10
Operating, delivery, and laboratories	20
Cystoscopic room	
General	100
Cystoscopic table	2500
Electroencephalographic suite	
Office	100
Workroom	30
Patients' room	30
Emergency room	
General	100
Local	2000
EKG, BMR and Specimen room	
General	20
Specimen table (supplementary)	50
Examination and treatment room	
General	50
Examining table	100
Lobby	30
Nurses' station	
General	20
Desk and charts	50
Medicine room counter	100
Nurses' workroom	30
Nurseries	
General	10

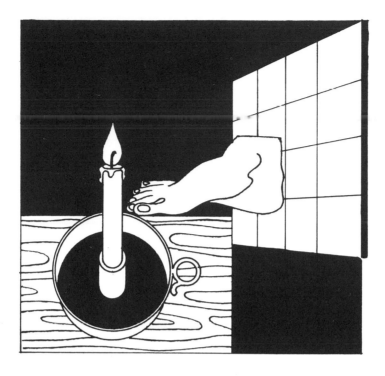

Examination table 70
Play room, pediatric 30

Obstetrical
    Clean-up, scrub-up rooms 30
    Labor room 20
    Delivery room, general 100
    Delivery table 2500

Pharmacy
    General 30
    Work table 100

Private rooms and wards
    General 10
    Reading 30

Radioisotope facilities
    Radiochemical laboratory 30
    Up-take measuring room 20
    Examination table 50

Surgery
    Operating room, general 100
    Operating table 2500

Waiting room
    General 15
    Reading 30

X-ray room and facilities 10-30

HOTELS

Guest rooms 10-30
Corridors, elevators and stairs 20
Entrance foyer 30
Front office 50
Lobby 10-30

OFFICES

General
    Cartography, designing, detailed drafting 200
    Accounting, bookkeeping, etc. 150
    Regular office work 100
    Reading 30-70
    Corridors, elevators, escalators, stairways 20

PUBLIC BUILDINGS (FIRE, POLICE, AND POST OFFICES)

Police
    Identification records 150
    Jail cells and interrogation rooms 30

Fire Hall
    Dormitory 20
    Recreation room 30

Post Offices
    Lobby, on tables 30
    Sorting, mailing, etc. 100
    Storage 20
    Corridors and stairways 20

RESTAURANTS, LUNCH ROOMS, CAFETERIAS

Cashier 50
Intimate type 10-3
Leisure type 30-15
Quick serivce type 100-50

Kitchen, commercial
    Inspection, checking and pricing 70
    Other areas 30

SCHOOLS

Reading printed material 30
Reading pencil writing 70

Spirit duplicated material
    Good 30
    Poor 100

Drafting, benchwork 100
Lip reading, chalkboards, sewing 150

STORES

Show windows
    Daytime lighting
        General 200
        Feature 1000
    Nighttime lighting
        Main business districts—highly competitive
            General 200
            Feature 1000
        Secondary business districts or small towns
            General 100
            Feature 500

Store interiors
    Circulation areas 30
    Merchandising areas
        Service 100
        Self-service 200
    Showcases and wall cases
        Service 200
        Self-service 500
    Feature displays
        Service 500
        Self-service 1000

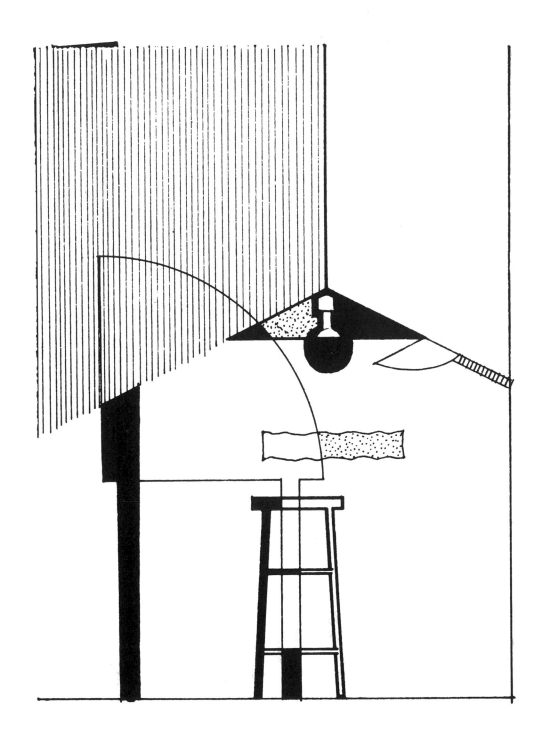

IN THE OFFICE

The small abstraction at left symbolizes one of the high points of yesterday's office lighting. A close inspection of Nino's sketch will reveal the profile of a roll-top desk, a hanging incandescent lamp with green shade and visor to match, and an elastic garter for shirt sleeve support. This sort of arrangement constituted a kind of Russian roulette in that the office worker of the time never knew whether his productivity would be terminated by heat prostration or blindness.

One of the most recent significant advances in office lighting is the development of the use of polarized light. The most common application of this form of lighting until the present was in sun glasses. It is now being utilized indoors to reduce glare and improve visibility of color. The method most commonly used to produce polarized light is to pass it through glass-flake panes where it is polarized by reorganization of the rays allowing only those rays to pass through that vibrate in the same direction. Another advantage in the use of polarizing panels is that when viewed at a normal angle the appearance is that of low brightness.

One of the problems in luminous ceiling installations is insuring a uniformity of brightness. Depending on the diffusing panel selected, certain ratios between lamp spacing (x) and height from panel (y) must be maintained.

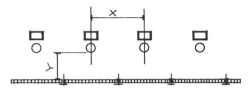

These ratios are usually suggested by the manufacturer of the panels and usually vary from a 1 to 1 to a 2 to 1 proportion.

The sketches on the next few pages show four of the most common types of diffusing panels: aluminum or plastic open egg crate, pre-formed vinyl diffusers, corrugated plastic sheets, and flat plastic sheets.

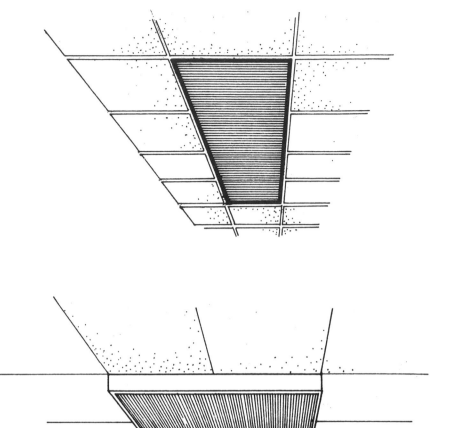

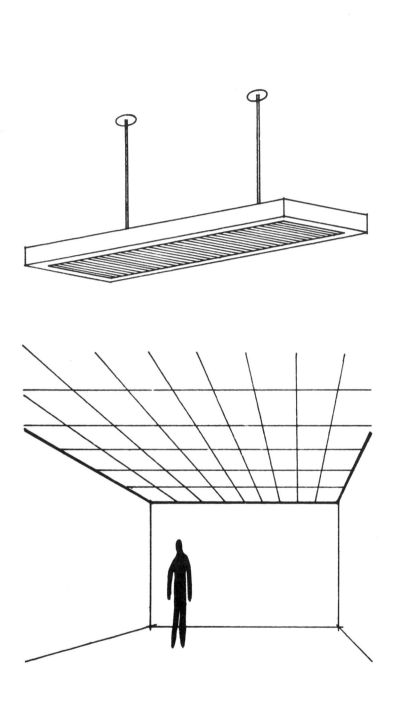

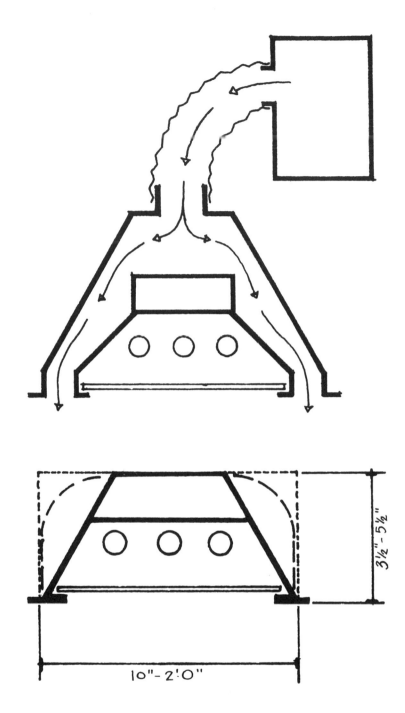

Today's general office areas are usually illuminated by recessed fluorescent troffer lighting shown at left, above, surface mounted fluorescent fixtures shown at left, below, or pendant mounted fixtures shown at top, center. Complete luminous ceiling installations as shown immediately above are also quite common. The sketches on the following pages show some basic dimensions and sizes.

The sketch at the top shows a recessed troffer type fixture that is combined with the air conditioning system and allows for the passage of supply air as well as illumination requirements while immediately above is a sketch showing a similar type troffer fixture. In broken lines are shown other typical silhouettes.

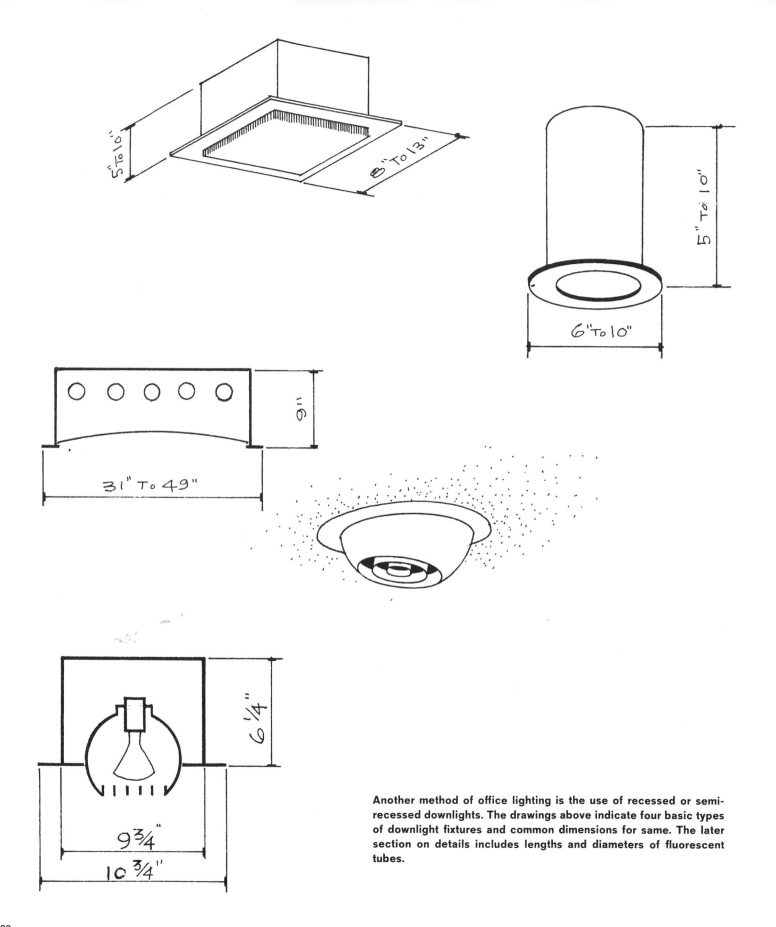

5" To 10"

6" To 13"

5" To 10"

6" To 10"

9"

31" To 49"

6 1/4"

9 3/4"

10 3/4"

Another method of office lighting is the use of recessed or semi-recessed downlights. The drawings above indicate four basic types of downlight fixtures and common dimensions for same. The later section on details includes lengths and diameters of fluorescent tubes.

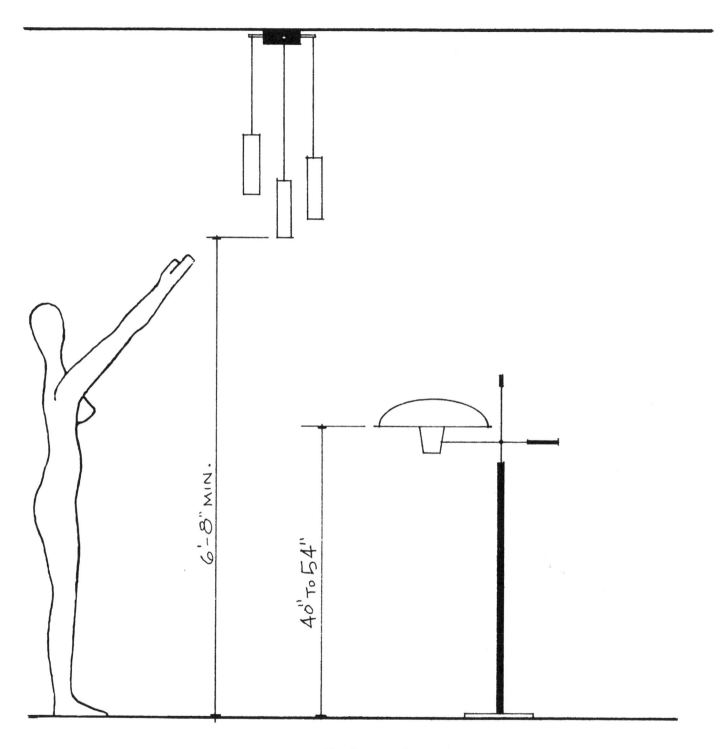

6'-8" MIN.

40" TO 54"

The drawings above indicate minimum heights for floor lamps and chandeliers above the floor. Unless it is intended that the client wear the fixtures shown, care should be exercised to respect clearances involved.

AT HOME

The following drawings represent several sneaky methods of handling lighting in the home. There is one important design factor, however, common to all three schemes. In all cases the measurements of the extensions in front of the lighting must be such as adequately to conceal the light source from view.

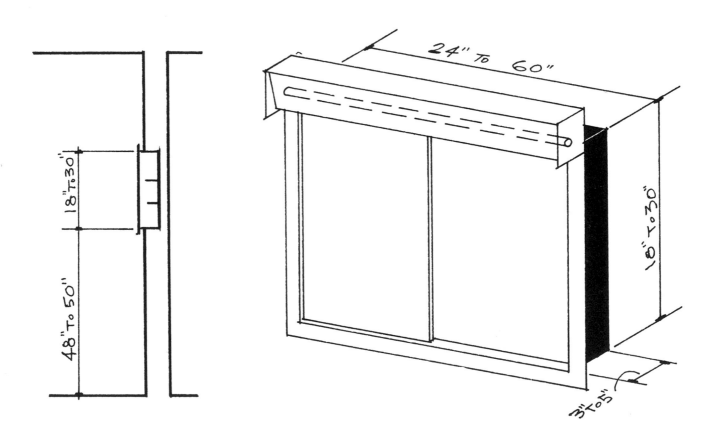

Medicine cabinets today come equipped with their own lighting and convenience outlets built-in. The sketches indicate the range of sizes available while the section at left shows suggested heights above the floor.

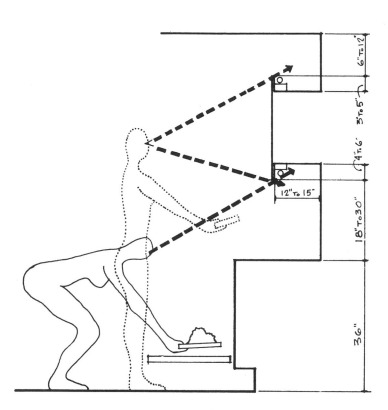

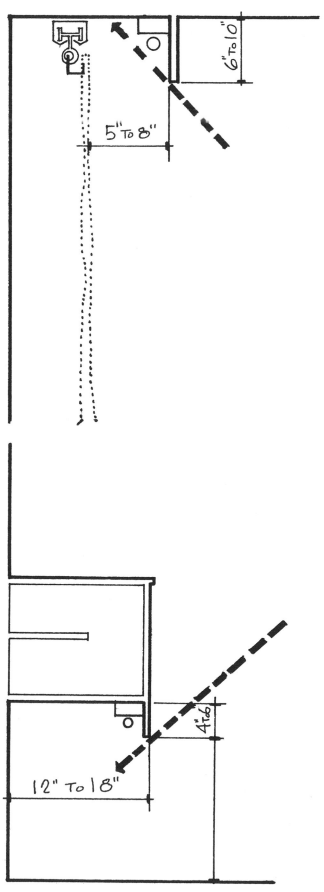

The drawing immediately above shows a method of providing lighting at a kitchen work center while the drawing at right, above, shows a possible valance lighting installation. The third drawing is a section through a hanging cabinet.

DETAILS

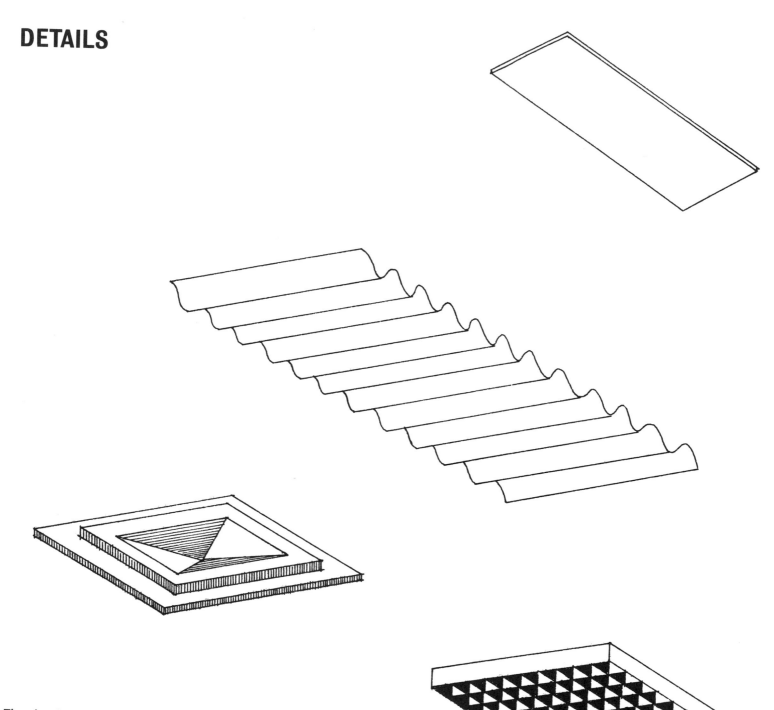

The sketch at right suggests an aluminum open egg crate type panel. This type is also usually available in color stabilized polystyrene plastic variations with open or closed hexagonal or square cells. Panel sizes are usually 2' x 2' or 2' x 4'. Another type is the pre-formed vinyl diffuser, shown immediately above, shaped in a variety of patterns. Most common sizes are 2' x 2', 2' x 3', and 2' x 4'. The other two figures show corrugated plastic and flat plastic or glass types. Corrugated sheets usually are supplied in rolls and the length may be cut to suit; roll width is usually 2'-0". Flat plastic or glass can be custom cut to suit.

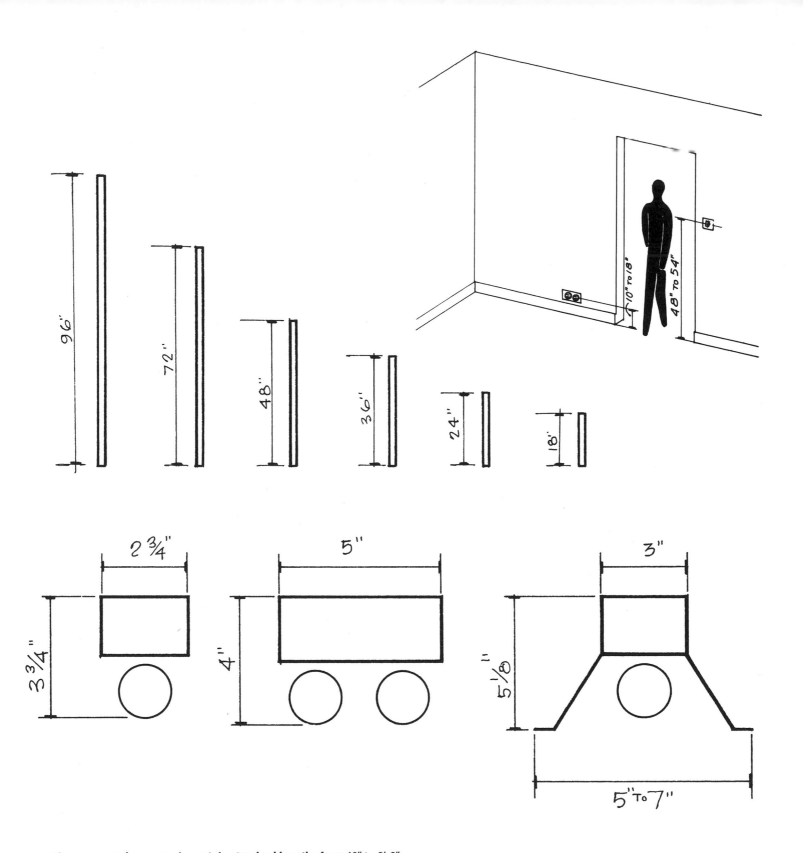

**Fluorescent tubes come in certain standard lengths from 18" to 8'-0"
while the fixtures themselves vary in dimensions as shown. These
dimensions are particularly useful for designing cove lighting.**

TABLES

CARPET AREA TABLES
(Based on standard 9′, 12′, 15′ & 18′ widths)

SQUARE FOOT TABLE
Feet and Inches Converted to Square Feet

INCHES	9′	12′	15′	18′	INCHES	9′	12′	15′	18′
1	.75	1.00	1.25	1.50	7	5.25	7.00	8.75	10.50
2	1.50	2.00	2.50	3.00	8	6.00	8.00	10.00	12.00
3	2.25	3.00	3.75	4.50	9	6.75	9.00	11.25	13.50
4	3.00	4.00	5.00	6.00	10	7.50	10.00	12.50	15.00
5	3.75	5.00	6.25	7.50	11	8.25	11.00	13.75	16.50
6	4.50	6.00	7.50	9.00					

Feet	9′	12′	15′	18′	Feet	9′	12′	15′	18′
1	9.00	12.00	15.00	18.00	36	324.00	432.00	540.00	648.00
2	18.00	24.00	30.00	36.00	37	333.00	444.00	555.00	666.00
3	27.00	36.00	45.00	54.00	38	342.00	456.00	570.00	684.00
4	36.00	48.00	60.00	72.00	39	351.00	468.00	585.00	702.00
5	45.00	60.00	75.00	90.00	40	360.00	480.00	600.00	720.00
6	54.00	72.00	90.00	108.00					
7	63.00	84.00	105.00	126.00	41	369.00	492.00	615.00	788.00
8	72.00	96.00	120.00	144.00	42	378.00	504.00	630.00	756.00
9	81.00	108.00	135.00	162.00	43	387.00	516.00	645.00	774.00
10	90.00	120.00	150.00	180.00	44	396.00	528.00	660.00	792.00
					45	405.00	540.00	675.00	810.00
11	99.00	132.00	165.00	198.00	46	414.00	552.00	690.00	828.00
12	108.00	144.00	180.00	216.00	47	423.00	564.00	705.00	846.00
13	117.00	156.00	195.00	234.00	48	432.00	576.00	720.00	864.00
14	126.00	168.00	210.00	252.00	49	441.00	588.00	735.00	882.00
15	135.00	180.00	225.00	270.00	50	450.00	600.00	750.00	900.00
16	144.00	192.00	240.00	288.00					
17	153.00	204.00	255.00	306.00	51	459.00	612.00	765.00	918.00
18	162.00	216.00	270.00	324.00	52	468.00	624.00	780.00	936.00
19	171.00	228.00	285.00	342.00	53	477.00	636.00	795.00	954.00
20	180.00	240.00	300.00	360.00	54	486.00	648.00	810.00	972.00
					55	495.00	660.00	825.00	990.00
21	189.00	252.00	315.00	378.00	56	504.00	672.00	840.00	1008.00
22	198.00	264.00	330.00	396.00	57	513.00	684.00	855.00	1026.00
23	207.00	276.00	345.00	414.00	58	522.00	696.00	870.00	1044.00
24	216.00	288.00	360.00	432.00	59	531.00	708.00	885.00	1062.00
25	225.00	300.00	375.00	450.00	60	540.00	720.00	900.00	1080.00
26	234.00	312.00	390.00	468.00					
27	243.00	324.00	405.00	486.00	61	549.00	732.00	915.00	1098.00
28	252.00	336.00	420.00	504.00	62	558.00	744.00	930.00	1116.00
29	261.00	348.00	435.00	522.00	63	567.00	756.00	945.00	1134.00
30	270.00	360.00	450.00	540.00	64	576.00	768.00	960.00	1152.00
					65	585.00	780.00	975.00	1170.00
31	279.00	372.00	465.00	558.00	66	594.00	792.00	990.00	1188.00
32	288.00	384.00	480.00	576.00	67	603.00	804.00	1005.00	1206.00
33	297.00	396.00	495.00	594.00	68	612.00	816.00	1020.00	1224.00
34	306.00	408.00	510.00	612.00	69	621.00	828.00	1035.00	1242.00
35	315.00	420.00	525.00	630.00	70	630.00	840.00	1050.00	1260.00

Example — 37′7″ of 12′ width

37′	=	444 sq. ft.
7″	=	7 sq. ft.
Total	=	451 sq. ft.

SQUARE YARD TABLE
Feet and Inches Converted to Square Yards

INCHES	9'	12'	15'	18'	INCHES	9'	12'	15'	18'
1	.08	.11	.14	.17	7	.58	.78	.97	1.17
2	.17	.22	.28	.33	8	.67	.89	1.11	1.34
3	.25	.33	.42	.50	9	.75	1.00	1.25	1.50
4	.33	.44	.56	.67	10	.83	1.11	1.39	1.67
5	.42	.55	.70	.83	11	.92	1.22	1.53	1.83
6	.50	.67	.84	1.00					

Feet	9'	12'	15'	18'	Feet	9'	12'	15'	18'
1	1.00	1.33	1.67	2.00	36	36.00	48.00	60.00	72.00
2	2.00	2.67	3.33	4.00	37	37.00	49.33	61.67	74.00
3	3.00	4.00	5.00	6.00	38	38.00	50.67	63.33	76.00
4	4.00	5.33	6.67	8.00	39	39.00	52.00	65.00	78.00
5	5.00	6.67	8.33	10.00	40	40.00	53.33	66.67	80.00
6	6.00	8.00	10.00	12.00					
7	7.00	9.33	11.67	14.00	41	41.00	54.67	68.33	82.00
8	8.00	10.67	13.33	16.00	42	42.00	56.00	70.00	84.00
9	9.00	12.00	15.00	18.00	43	43.00	57.33	71.67	86.00
10	10.00	13.33	16.67	20.00	44	44.00	58.67	73.33	88.00
					45	45.00	60.00	75.00	90.00
11	11.00	14.67	18.33	22.00	46	46.00	61.33	76.67	92.00
12	12.00	16.00	20.00	24.00	47	47.00	62.67	78.33	94.00
13	13.00	17.33	21.67	26.00	48	48.00	64.00	80.00	96.00
14	14.00	18.67	23.33	28.00	49	49.00	65.33	81.67	98.00
15	15.00	20.00	25.00	30.00	50	50.00	66.67	83.33	100.00
16	16.00	21.33	26.67	32.00					
17	17.00	22.67	28.33	34.00	51	51.00	68.00	85.00	102.00
18	18.00	24.00	30.00	36.00	52	52.00	69.33	86.67	104.00
19	19.00	25.33	31.67	38.00	53	53.00	70.67	88.33	106.00
20	20.00	26.67	33.33	40.00	54	54.00	72.00	90.00	108.00
					55	55.00	73.33	91.67	110.00
21	21.00	28.00	35.00	42.00	56	56.00	74.67	93.33	112.00
22	22.00	29.33	36.67	44.00	57	57.00	76.00	95.00	114.00
23	23.00	30.67	38.33	46.00	58	58.00	77.33	96.67	116.00
24	24.00	32.00	40.00	48.00	59	59.00	78.67	98.33	118.00
25	25.00	33.33	41.67	50.00	60	60.00	80.00	100.00	120.00
26	26.00	34.67	43.33	52.00					
27	27.00	36.00	45.00	54.00	61	61.00	81.33	101.67	122.00
28	28.00	37.33	46.67	56.00	62	62.00	82.67	103.33	124.00
29	29.00	38.67	48.33	58.00	63	63.00	84.00	105.00	126.00
30	30.00	40.00	50.00	60.00	64	64.00	85.33	106.67	128.00
					65	65.00	86.67	108.33	130.00
31	31.00	41.33	51.67	62.00	66	66.00	88.00	110.00	132.00
32	32.00	42.67	53.33	64.00	67	67.00	89.33	111.67	134.00
33	33.00	44.00	55.00	66.00	68	68.00	90.67	113.33	136.00
34	34.00	45.33	56.67	68.00	69	69.00	92.00	115.00	138.00
35	35.00	46.67	58.33	70.00	70	70.00	93.33	116.67	140.00

Example — 48'3" of 12' width

48' = 64 sq. yds.
3" = .33
Total = 64.33 sq. yds.

CEILING AND FLOOR TILE QUANTITIES FORMULAS

TILE SIZE IN INCHES	TILE QUANTITY FORMULA
6x6	$\dfrac{L \times W}{4}$ = NUMBER OF TILES
9x9	$\dfrac{L \times W \times 16}{9}$ = NUMBER OF TILES
12x12	$L \times W$ = NUMBER OF TILES
12x24	$\dfrac{L \times W}{2}$ = NUMBER OF TILES
12x36	$\dfrac{L \times W}{3}$ = NUMBER OF TILES
12x48	$\dfrac{L \times W}{4}$ = NUMBER OF TILES
16x16	$\dfrac{L \times W}{16}$ = NUMBER OF TILES
18x36	$\dfrac{L \times W \times 2}{9}$ = NUMBER OF TILES
24x24	$\dfrac{L \times W}{4}$ = NUMBER OF TILES
24x36	$\dfrac{L \times W}{6}$ = NUMBER OF TILES
24x48	$\dfrac{L \times W}{8}$ = NUMBER OF TILES
24x60	$\dfrac{L \times W}{10}$ = NUMBER OF TILES

L = Length of floor or ceiling in feet.
W = Width of floor or ceiling in feet.

PROPERTIES OF THE CIRCLE

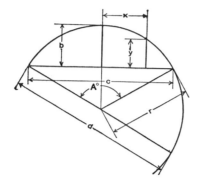

Circumference $= 6.28318\ r = 3.14159\ d$
Diameter $= 0.31831$ circumference
Area $= 3.14159\ r^2$

Arc $\quad a = \dfrac{\pi r\ A°}{180°} = 0.017453\ r\ A°$

Angle $A° = \dfrac{180°\ a}{\pi r} = 57.29578\ \dfrac{a}{r}$

Radius $r = \dfrac{4\ b^2 + c^2}{8\ b}$

Chord $c = 2\sqrt{2\ br - b^2} = 2\ r \sin \dfrac{A}{2}$

Rise $\quad b = r - \tfrac{1}{2}\sqrt{4\ r^2 - c^2} = \dfrac{c}{2} \tan \dfrac{A}{4}$

$\qquad\qquad = 2\ r \sin^2 \dfrac{A}{4} = r + y - \sqrt{r^2 - x^2}$

$y = b - r + \sqrt{r^2 - x^2}$

$x = \sqrt{r^2 - (r + y - b)^2}$

Diameter of circle of equal periphery as square $= 1.27324$ side of square
Side of square of equal periphery as circle $= 0.78540$ diameter of circle
Diameter of circle circumscribed about square $= 1.41421$ side of square
Side of square inscribed in circle $= 0.70711$ diameter of circle

---

CIRCULAR SECTOR

$r =$ radius of circle $\qquad y =$ angle ncp in degrees

Area of Sector ncpo $= \tfrac{1}{2}$ (length of arc nop $\times$ r)

$\qquad\qquad = $ Area of Circle $\times \dfrac{y}{360}$

$\qquad\qquad = 0.0087266 \times r^2 \times y$

CIRCULAR SEGMENT

$r =$ radius of circle $\qquad x =$ chord $\qquad b =$ rise

Area of Segment nop $=$ Area of Sector ncpo $-$ Area of triangle ncp

$\qquad = \dfrac{(\text{Length of arc nop} \times r) - x\ (r - b)}{2}$

Area of Segment nsp $=$ Area of Circle $-$ Area of Segment nop

---

VALUES FOR FUNCTIONS OF π

$\pi = 3.14159265359, \qquad \log = 0.4971499$

$\pi^2 = 9.8696044,\ \log = 0.9942997 \quad \dfrac{1}{\pi} = 0.3183099,\ \log = \overline{1}.5028501 \quad \sqrt{\dfrac{1}{\pi}} = 0.5641896,\ \log = \overline{1}.7514251$

$\pi^3 = 31.0062767,\ \log = 1.4914496 \quad \dfrac{1}{\pi^2} = 0.1013212,\ \log = \overline{1}.0057003 \quad \dfrac{\pi}{180} = 0.0174533,\ \log = \overline{2}.2418774$

$\sqrt{\pi} = 1.7724539,\ \log = 0.2485749 \quad \dfrac{1}{\pi^3} = 0.0322515,\ \log = \overline{2}.5085500 \quad \dfrac{180}{\pi} = 57.2957795,\ \log = 1.7581226$

DECIMALS OF A FOOT FOR EACH 32ND OF AN INCH

Inch	0″	1″	2″	3″	4″	5″
0	0	.0833	.1667	.2500	.3333	.4167
1/32	.0026	.0859	.1693	.2526	.3359	.4193
1/16	.0052	.0885	.1719	.2552	.3385	.4219
3/32	.0078	.0911	.1745	.2578	.3411	.4245
1/8	.0104	.0938	.1771	.2604	.3438	.4271
5/32	.0130	.0964	.1797	.2630	.3464	.4297
3/16	.0156	.0990	.1823	.2656	.3490	.4323
7/32	.0182	.1016	.1849	.2682	.3516	.4349
1/4	.0208	.1042	.1875	.2708	.3542	.4375
9/32	.0234	.1068	.1901	.2734	.3568	.4401
5/16	.0260	.1094	.1927	.2760	.3594	.4427
11/32	.0286	.1120	.1953	.2786	.3620	.4453
3/8	.0313	.1146	.1979	.2812	.3646	.4479
13/32	.0339	.1172	.2005	.2839	.3672	.4505
7/16	.0365	.1198	.2031	.2865	.3698	.4531
15/32	.0391	.1224	.2057	.2891	.3724	.4557
1/2	.0417	.1250	.2083	.2917	.3750	.4583
17/32	.0443	.1276	.2109	.2943	.3776	.4609
9/16	.0469	.1302	.2135	.2969	.3802	.4635
19/32	.0495	.1328	.2161	.2995	.3928	.4661
5/8	.0521	.1354	.2188	.3021	.3854	.4688
21/32	.0547	.1380	.2214	.3047	.3880	.4714
11/16	.0573	.1406	.2240	.3073	.3906	.4740
23/32	.0599	.1432	.2266	.3099	.3932	.4766
3/4	.0625	.1458	.2292	.3125	.3958	.4792
25/32	.0651	.1484	.2318	.3151	.3984	.4818
13/16	.0677	.1510	.2344	.3177	.4010	.4844
27/32	.0703	.1536	.2370	.3203	.4036	.4870
7/8	.0729	.1563	.2396	.3229	.4063	.4896
29/32	.0755	.1589	.2422	.3255	.4089	.4922
15/16	.0781	.1615	.2448	.3281	.4115	.4948
31/32	.0807	.1641	.2474	.3307	.4141	.4974

DECIMALS OF A FOOT FOR EACH 32ND OF AN INCH

Inch	6″	7″	8″	9″	10″	11″
0	.5000	.5833	.6667	.7500	.8333	.9167
1/32	.5026	.5859	.6693	.7526	.8359	.9193
1/16	.5052	.5885	.6719	.7552	.8385	.9219
3/32	.5078	.5911	.6745	.7578	.8411	.9245
1/8	.5104	.5938	.6771	.7604	.8438	.9271
5/32	.5130	.5964	.6797	.7630	.8464	.9297
3/16	.5156	.5990	.6823	.7656	.8490	.9323
7/32	.5182	.6016	.6849	.7682	.8516	.9349
1/4	.5208	.6042	.6875	.7708	.8542	.9375
9/32	.5234	.6068	.6901	.7734	.8568	.9401
5/16	.5260	.6094	.6927	.7760	.8594	.9427
11/32	.5286	.6120	.6953	.7786	.8620	.9453
3/8	.5313	.6146	.6979	.7813	.8646	.9479
13/32	.5339	.6172	.7005	.7839	.8672	.9505
7/16	.5365	.6198	.7031	.7865	.8698	.9531
15/32	.5391	.6224	.7057	.7891	.8724	.9557
1/2	.5417	.6250	.7083	.7917	.8750	.9583
17/32	.5443	.6276	.7109	.7943	.8776	.9609
9/16	.5469	.6302	.7135	.7969	.8802	.9635
19/32	.5495	.6328	.7161	.7995	.8828	.9661
5/8	.5521	.6354	.7188	.8021	.8854	.9688
21/32	.5547	.6380	.7214	.8047	.8880	.9714
11/16	.5573	.6406	.7240	.8073	.8906	.9740
23/32	.5599	.6432	.7266	.8099	.8932	.9766
3/4	.5625	.6458	.7292	.8125	.8958	.9792
25/32	.5651	.6484	.7318	.8151	.8984	.9818
13/16	.5677	.6510	.7344	.8177	.9010	.9844
27/32	.5703	.6536	.7370	.8203	.9036	.9870
7/8	.5729	.6563	.7396	.8229	.9063	.9896
29/32	.5755	.6589	.7422	.8255	.9089	.9922
15/16	.5781	.6615	.7448	.8281	.9115	.9948
31/32	.5807	.6641	.7474	.8307	.9141	.9974

UNITED STATES AND METRIC SYSTEMS OF MEASURE

UNITED STATES SYSTEM

LINEAR

12 inches	=	1 foot
3 feet	=	1 yard
5½ yards	=	1 rod
40 rods	=	1 furlong
8 furlongs	=	1 mile
		(5,280 ft.)

SQUARE

144 sq. inches	=	1 sq. foot
9 sq. ft.	=	1 sq. yard
30¼ sq. yards	=	1 sq. rod
160 sq. rods	=	1 acre
640 acres	=	1 sq. mile

METRIC SYSTEM

LENGTH

1 kilometer	=	1,000 meters	= 3,280 feet, 10 inches
1 hectometer	=	100 meters	= 328 feet, 1 inch
1 meter	=	1 meter	= 39.37 inches
1 centimeter	=	.01 meter	= .3937 inch
1 millimeter	=	.001 meter	= .0394 inch
1 micron	=	.000001 meter	= .000039 inch
1 millimicron	=	.000000001 meter	= .000000039 inch

SURFACE

1 sq. kilometer	=	1,000,000 sq. meters	= .3861 sq. mile
1 hectare	=	10,000 sq. meters	= 2.47 acres
1 are	=	100 sq. meters	= 119.6 sq. yards
1 centare	=	1 sq. meter	= 1,550 sq. inches
1 sq. centimeter	=	.0001 sq. meter	= .155 sq. inch
1 sq. millimeter	=	.000001 sq. meter	= .00155 sq. inch